Me, God a...

Tools for tough times

Dorothy Jane Neilson

GILEAD
B O O K S
PUBLISHING

Gilead Books Publishing
Corner Farm
West Knapton
Malton
North Yorkshire YO17 8JB UK
www.GileadBooksPublishing.com

First published in Great Britain, March 2014
2 4 6 8 10 9 7 5 3 1

British Library Cataloguing in Publication Data:
A CIP catalogue record for this book is available from the British
Library.

ISBN-13: 978-0-9926713-1-0

The publisher makes every effort to ensure that the papers used in
our books are made from trees that have been legally sourced from
well-managed and credibly certified forests by using a printer
awarded FSC & PEFC chain of custody certification.

Cover design: Nathan Ward
Cover illustration: Anna Tash

To Peter, whose unconditional love
helped make me whole.

To my daughters, Pauline, Jane and Susan, whose
love means everything to me.

And to my dear friends Janet and Maggie
whose desire for my friendship,
even through the depression years,
will always be a mystery to me.

Contents

Introduction
The White Staircase

The auditorium was hushed in expectancy. Four hundred people were waiting. I took a very deep breath, commanded my muscles to stop shaking and spoke into the silence.

'Fake it till you make it,' was the mantra of the day. They don't know how nervous you are, I told myself. Look confident. Sound confident. You know your stuff. Get on and do it. You CAN do this. You are an expert, waiting to be discovered! This stage has been waiting for you for twenty years. This is your brand new beginning—the birth of tomorrow.

Somehow on that stage on a March evening, a frog was turning into a princess. A dream was becoming a reality and a curse was being broken. If there was a sound other than my hammering heart it was only the taunts of the past sounding a distant note somewhere in the wings. And if the light was patchy it was just the shadows of self-doubt and fear that still followed me around. But under that spotlight in that auditorium stood a new creation, one that had emerged over years from a block of frozen, petrified stone which deep inside held the real me; the fledgling that was testing her wings in public that night for the first time.

The audience was kind. For them I was just another speaker. They had no idea that what they were witnessing was a birth. They had endured a staggering number of teachers and facilitators throughout the course of the week and, quite frankly, they were ready to retreat to the bar for an hour and then to bed. But they thanked me warmly—and moved on—to their coffee or their beers or to catch up with their phone calls.

And I hid behind the stage curtain until the silence assured me that I was alone and it was safe to come out.

Of course I was much too old to be behaving like a scared schoolgirl and I knew it. But that night was so important to me. I had lived the last fifteen years of my life in the grip of depression, energy-guzzling and confidence sapping, claustrophobic and debilitating, deadening and saddening, and so paralysing that I believed that never again would I experience any quality of life. The slow crawl back to the real world had been horrid, up the ladder one day, waving to the world and anticipating the fun of joining in and the next day back down in the dungeon of failure where emotion didn't exist apart from the black wallpaper of sadness that wrapped itself around, sucking all life into itself.

It was different back then, in another world, before depression, when youth and enthusiasm dreamed its dream and I was going to amount to something. Nothing great, you understand. But I would be fun and whacky and I would move in fun and whacky circles and I would be loved and respected and people would want to be with me and they would think I was wise and funny and I would have a place there with them. When I was a young, carefree girl with the whole of time and geography ahead of me I lived in anticipation of a fair and honest world where we would all try our hardest to make our own orbit perfect. And we would succeed.

In becoming a teacher I would pass on all my wisdom—and a little of my arrogance—to my young charges and they would lend their weight in making the world a perfect place. In committing myself to the Christian cause as a teenager I was asking God to do his bit as well. In marrying a perfect man—well, of course, he WOULD be perfect! He had his ideals too and together we would be mighty! I was all set to make a difference to the world, take it out of the mess that millions of people had made and live the rest of my life just enjoying its beauty.

It's interesting to go back to those days and see what a perfectionist I was. And see how simplistic my ideals were, and how impractical they proved to be. How could I do anything other than fail when I started out with these simple aims for my life—just to make the world perfect. That's all. Nothing more or less would do. The world had to be put right. And I would do it— in my school, in my spare time activities, in my marriage and in my tiny new family as each of my daughters arrived. They too would be perfect (actually, they were and still are, but don't tell the world. They won't believe me.)

As I stood on my principles, strong, arrogant and determined, gradually the ocean invaded my space and began to wash away the foundations of my idealism and I began to crumble. Not all at once. No great landslide into the sea. No avalanche for everybody to gawp at, but a slow eroding of my confidence. The world was not changing. People were not trying to make the world better. Nobody seemed to appreciate that I knew and that I was right and that my way would work. I began to realise that it was not a perfect world. The God I had thought was all wise and powerful and also wanted a perfect world was just not playing the game.

My strategy had been that if I was kind to people they would be kind to me. If I loved people they would love me. If I was fair, others would be fair to me. I was wrong. The world didn't play according to my rules. I began to feel as if I was drowning.

I could not live in this world.

When I was in my thirties I began to realise that I had painted myself into a corner and there was nowhere to go. I wasn't ready at that time to go into meltdown. Not yet. I was still struggling. Maybe I could salvage something out of my ideals. Start again perhaps, miles away from the scene of my crumbling perfectionism. A fresh start with new people who might know another way to live. I could learn.

I love my bed. I've always loved my bed. Sleep is a great comfort to me, the deeper the better, hours and hours of it. Zzzzzzz

That night it was a white staircase. Very similar to the green one I had in a previous dream. Painted pure white, a matt paint, walls and ceiling and treads all the same brilliant white. It seemed newly painted, no dust, no footmarks spoiling the freshness. And just like the green stair of a few nights ago it was useless. It didn't go anywhere. I climbed up, hoping, anticipating. In the dream I saw it as a way out of my world, my trap where it had all gone wrong. I could escape to a different world. It was easy after all. You just climb the staircase and enter another place, a new room where it will all be different. An Alice in Wonderland place, or Narnia, or Hogwarts. My life could change and I would have a fresh start.

But again I reached the blank ceiling. Thumping on it didn't help. It was, as it looked, a ceiling—a white, solid ceiling. There was no going anywhere through that ceiling. The end of the way out. No way out. Stuck at the top of the stair to nowhere. Trapped.

Sulking there on the top step, I realised that there just might be a way after all. On the wall there was a very small wooden door—very Alice in Wonderland— like a trapdoor. So I opened it and began to squeeze through it into the next world. The world out there was vibrant, the laughter hitting me immediately and I felt my mood lift at the sound of it. As I stuck my head through the trapdoor I realised that I was looking into a darkened theatre, filled with people enjoying themselves. I could see the stage down on my left and I tried to squeeze my body through the gap, flesh fighting and scraping against wood and plaster. This was exciting. I was going to enjoy this new world.

But alas, my body was too big. I was being allowed a tantalising glimpse of this exciting new dimension of living but was unable to get out there and experience it. But for almost twenty years I held the memory of that dream and light years of experience later I had entered into that reality, stood on that stage and began life in that new dimension.

Dreams do come true. But the frog took a lifetime to turn into the princess. Magic seems not to be instantaneous. In fact, in retrospect, I see that the road is littered with the tools I needed to hack my way through the forest and get to that stage in Aviemore. Valuable tools, many of them ancient and had to be rediscovered. Many others were hand-crafted as the need arose. Others were passed on from wise people. Tools for a journey from one form of life to another. Tools that will be offered to you in this book.

Tools for tough times.

Dorothy Neilson
March 2014

Chapter 1

Meltdown

The path ahead was steep, winding its way through the trees and rocks. Underfoot the going was rough over stones and tree roots. But the shade was welcome. I began to think that I should do this more often, enjoy the lovely surroundings and even get fit again. It had been a long time since I had done any form of exercise, our poor dog having to content himself with short sniffs around the streets. But for some unknown reason the warm September sun had tempted me out today and I was making my first excursion into the local beauty spots. The scenery was outstanding, the air was exhilarating and I realised how much I had missed the freedom of my long walks.

My heart was thudding in my chest and I was even beginning to feel a little light-headed. How unfit must I be after all these months cooped up in the house. But, now enthusiastic and determined, I forced myself on and soon came unexpectedly out of the shade and into the brilliance of the sunshine. Ahead was moorland and a vast expanse of purple heather stretching like a royal carpet towards the horizon.

Somewhere close by, a curlew cried and flew up from the stillness of the moor. Then all was enveloped in silence again. I stopped briefly and looked around me, drinking in the beauty and peace of that spot. Another fifty yards took me to the summit and I gladly sank onto an exposed rock and let my exhausted limbs relax.

Far below me the strath snoozed in the afternoon heat and I could make out the grey ribbon of road that ran between Crieff and Comrie and the little mound with its monument, which I could see from my bedroom window. Beyond that, the real mountains started and in the distance the dark peaks seemed much more menacing than the rolling foothills I had ventured into today. It was all so peaceful. Why had I never done this before, I was asking myself? Why had I kept myself a prisoner in the house all this time?

Home had been in this sleepy little Perthshire town for more than a year now. The change from the bustle of the city to this quiet tourist centre had been difficult and I still couldn't say I was exactly happy in my new home. My husband was happy. The new job was busy and rewarding and he loved the challenge. For his sake I really wanted to make it work. But I missed Edinburgh desperately and felt that I grieved the loss of my old life every single day.

Gazing south at the distant Lomond Hills I realised that Edinburgh was just over the horizon, just out of sight. And the sick feeling of homesickness gripped me again. I was living in exile, far from home, far from my friends, far from all that gave me life. And I felt the energy drain out of me as I sank back into a dull place of weariness, where there was only deep sadness.

Our faithful spaniel settled down beside me, also tired from his climb, and I stroked his ears, reliving in my mind's eye that awful day when all this began.

It started on a Saturday. For our three daughters and me it was a special Saturday because Scotland was playing rugby against a depleted Welsh team and we might just have a chance of winning. We were looking forward to the match on television that afternoon. Peter wasn't much of a rugby fan, but it amused him to watch his family's trauma as the game unfolded! So we all settled down in front of the television in anticipation of a close and exciting game. But that day, he missed the match completely because a colleague phoned him and he spent more than an hour discussing a possible change to his job which would involve moving to a new town.

Once our valiant Scottish team had won their match in spectacular form, Peter lost no time in telling us all about his conversation and how excited he was at the possible challenges of the proposed changes.

I don't think he had any idea of the devastation he left behind him when he returned to his office to prepare for a meeting. Three teenage girls all settled and happy in school, each with activities and friends and ambitions, each left feeling anxious and uneasy and even downright scared. And they weren't the only ones who were scared. My reaction was panic at the thought of moving—again. This was our fifth home. And this was where I wanted to stay. I had never felt more settled than in this place and I couldn't bear the thought of leaving.

DIARY ENTRY April 9th

Still having problems with the new move. Peter is so excited at all the possibilities. Even the girls are coming round now that they've seen the house and have chosen their new bedrooms. I still don't want to go!

April 12th

I finished work at lunchtime today and decided to take a walk and try to sort out my woolly head. I just can't come to terms with all this. I took the car round Arthur's Seat and parked at Dunsapie Loch, realising of course that I should have brought the dog and, more importantly, my wellies! However, it was too late for that and anyway, I just wanted to sit and think and the dog would have been too restless.

I just felt so miserable! I climbed as quickly as I could, both to keep warm and also to be positive. The wind was really strong at the top of the first slope so I turned right and went round the hill to the rocky part where I was a bit more sheltered. You get a great view of the city from there.

And sitting there, I really did try to sort things out rationally and decide that a move wouldn't be too bad. But the whole of my being was rebelling against my logic. Of course, moving job and house isn't the end of the world—but it sure felt like it at that moment.

I cried a lot. But maybe I'm just being selfish.

April 20th

I woke up this morning really angry. Why the heck should I go? I am one fifth of this family and if I want to stay in Edinburgh then why not? I should say all this, argue my case. I am NOT moving out of this place. I WANT TO STAY HERE!

April 23rd

Since I was nineteen I have wanted to put God first in my life. I wouldn't want to make any decision against what I believe to be what he wants. If he is 'calling us' out of here then I must go—no matter where that is. If he wants us in Crieff then we have to go there. He knows what the master plan is for us and all I need to do is trust him. Hmmm...sounds easier than it feels right now!

Looking back, I realise that I thought I had rationally worked it all out and accepted that this was the right thing to do. God doesn't call the breadwinner into a new, exciting job, totally disregarding the lives of the other family members. He calls us in families. If it is the right move for one member of the family, then he must also have plans for the others. But that day, climbing the Knock in the September sunshine, I was struggling to remember what happiness was. God was in this situation. It should be going well. We should all be happy. We should be functioning as the perfect family. How naïve!

The day of the move went well enough although it rained incessantly—maybe a warning of times to come. The gravel drive became a quagmire and the removal van was too wide to fit in the gate. All my furniture had to be carried piece by soggy piece through the puddles. And the new carpets were in severe danger from very large, dirty boots.

We finally got all our belongings out of the removal van, with very little help from me. My brain seemed to pack up and I became so fuzzy that I could no longer think clearly, nor plan, nor make lists, nor even answer simple questions. Peter seemed to take over and he masterminded all the unpacking in our new house while I wilted in the kitchen trying to feed a thousand helpers. Everyone was too cheerful, assuring me that I would love living in the country, once the rain stopped.

July 3rd

Well, we've arrived. I followed the removal van. Peter met the girls from school and brought them straight here, still tear-stained from their goodbyes. There's not much enthusiasm for this move. Pauline's ok. She'll stay with the Nicols next year and complete her schooling in Edinburgh. It seems to make more sense with only one year to go.

Jane is seriously in a huff. She wanted to stay in Edinburgh too but we said no. She will go to school here for her last two years. Susan—well, she had no choice. But she is just devastated. I feel as though I have had to use a crowbar to prise them out of Edinburgh.

The house is ok. Huge though. Half our stuff is in an enormous cupboard on the landing. The rooms look nice now, freshly decorated and a brand new kitchen. But it isn't home. I can't find a room where I can sit down and relax. It feels like a hotel—only not so clean and tidy!

I just feel so empty inside. Will I ever get used to this place?

July 6th

I am so tired. I hate this house. Yes, I know, it's a beautiful old house! And I know it cost a fortune. And I'm not being very grateful. But I don't feel grateful!

This is a stranger's house. And it is just so big—I will never have the energy to clean it. Our bedroom is really beautiful with a lovely view down the valley and the hills all silhouetted against the sky. But it isn't my bedroom. Went shopping today. Ghastly supermarket! And it was raining!!

July 7th

Pauline has gone to camp and the other two go off tomorrow. So we will be alone. Peter just loves the new job and is in his office every hour of the day. Although he does have an office in the house too so he works there in the evenings.

Maybe I will start the garden while they are away. The garden is enormous and a bit overgrown now since nothing has been done since last autumn. I haven't a clue where to start or even what to do. I've never done this before!

I sat on the back doorstep this morning in the sunshine. It is so quiet after Edinburgh. The trees were full of birds chirping and it was very peaceful. I did some thinking.

What was this all about? Did God want me to be unhappy? Did he even know that I was unhappy? I want to do the right thing—follow God's will. Surely God wouldn't say 'This is a great job for Peter. Sorry you will be miserable.' He wouldn't do that! So why does it feel all wrong, as if he doesn't care about me?

'God, this is a lot to ask of me. I loved my life in the city. I loved my house, my job, my routine, my friends, but I also love my husband. And I try to love you. So I thought I was doing my duty by moving here. I did it for you!

'So why am I so unhappy? Why don't you make it ok? I did this for you but now I feel as though you've abandoned me. You've brought me into this awful place in the middle of nowhere and you've just left me.

'There's no pat on the back, no 'well done, Dorothy, for being a big, brave girl', no words of comfort from the Bible, no nothing! I'm not asking for an earthquake or shooting stars in the night sky.

'I just want to know that you are still there and that I'm safe and secure in your care. I just feel so alone.'

July 13th

I have had to leave the comfort of the back door step coz it has been invaded by a million ants! Yuck!!

So I've been forced to start weeding the garden instead. Anything rather than stay indoors. 'Plant gardens,' God advised the Jews in Babylonia! And I did find a certain peace today, working away, pulling out the weeds. And it was great to see the difference at the end of an hour or two. I felt I had some control over something again. The rest of my world is so much out of control at the moment. But to be able to clear a patch of ground, shape it and plant it up again gave me a wonderful feeling of getting my life back on track. The feeling didn't last long. But it was a start!

The garden became my refuge after that. The joy of a new and strangely absorbing hobby took the edge off the pain of loneliness and dislocation that I was feeling. I discovered garden centres, where the plants were alluring and completely unknown to this novice. I knew so little that I turned to gardening programmes on television and tried to learn all I could about the condition of my soil, the difference between exotic weeds and commonplace flowers, what grew in which areas and the definition of annuals, perennials and herbs.

Garden Centres often had coffee shops and I found an oasis there within the sight and smell of growing things and far from my unfamiliar, unwelcoming house which became colder and colder as the season progressed. Another displacement activity was an upholstery class in a neighbouring village and an evening class on the history of the local area. But I carried the ever-present scent of sadness around with me and people left me alone to mourn.

Throughout the long, frosty winter I tried so hard to appear normal, whatever that was, trying to create and hold together a home for my family. But nothing was right. I lay awake for hours during the night, I lost my concentration so that reading was no longer a pleasure and I even resorted to buying gardening magazines so that I could look at the pictures and dream of warm days in the garden and plan all the improvements I would make next season.

All this time the snow lay thickly and the girls missed several days of school. Black ice was our constant companion. We slithered and slipped our way along the river path with the dog each day. Although even he was often reluctant to face the Perthshire weather! The tree at the end of the drive buckled under the weight of its snowy burden and blocked the drive and the main road for a whole day till we managed to cut it up into little pieces and trundle it into the coal cellar.

Our coal fire however failed to melt the ice within or without the house. The windows rattled, the wind howled through, straight from the North Pole and one particularly stormy night, the garage from across the road landed in our garden. The winding, country road which linked us to the motorway fifteen miles away became impassable and didn't seem to merit visits from the gritters. So we felt cut-off and isolated and Pauline couldn't get home for weekends from Edinburgh.

It didn't seem possible that things could get worse! Wrong!

The snow melted, the roads flooded, the central heating boiler broke down. One freezing morning I opened the curtains to discover that a starling had flown down the chimney during the night and had redecorated the room in soot while trying to escape. A neighbour complained that our overgrown bushes were ruining his garden and Susan slipped a disc and had to have an emergency operation in Dundee.

But slowly, slowly snow turned to rain and we began to notice the brave snowdrops poking their heads out of the soil. And hope rose within me as the days lengthened and spring turned into summer.

I had made it through the first winter!

To ponder:

> Day and night I cry, and tears are my only food; all the time my enemies ask me, 'Where is your God?'
>
> My heart breaks when I remember the past, when I went with the crowds to the house of God and led them as they walked along, a happy crowd, singing and shouting praise to God.
>
> Why am I so sad? Why am I so troubled? I will put my hope in God, and once again I will praise him, my saviour and my God.
>
> Here in exile my heart is breaking, and so I turn my thoughts to him. He has sent waves of sorrow over my soul; chaos roars at me like a flood,
>
> Why am I so sad? Why am I so troubled? I will put my hope in God, and once again I will praise him, my saviour and my God.
>
> (From Psalm 42)

Chapter 2

Loss

It's such a little, quiet word, almost a whisper. But it silently screams, out of the heart, a torrent of emptiness and hurt and meaningless pain. It can't be put into words at first. It doesn't even register on the emotional scale for a while. But for me, life just felt all wrong. Something sustaining and life-giving in my situation had been withheld and everything had changed. The ground had shifted under my feet. I was disorientated. I was muddled. Thinking was done through a filter. Physical movement seemed as difficult as climbing Mount Everest without oxygen. I was doing all the normal things. But I had become a different person.

Had one of Harry Potter's dementors attacked me in the middle of the night and sucked the soul out of me? Had I left the real me locked up in a cupboard in my old house and was I walking around without myself? Had I perhaps never existed in the first place but the batteries had run down on the fake and it had now been discarded? Dead—but still breathing?

Loss. We all experience it. Usually we recognise it when it happens. But just sometimes, it creeps up gradually and we miss the signs till it snowballs out of control and knocks us flat before we know what has happened to us. I had a string of losses at that time which I had energetically swept under the carpet feeling that if I didn't think about them, didn't let them feature in my positive thinking, then all would be well. Wrong! On the contrary, the huge lump in the carpet just tripped me up and I fell flat on my face.

So what had I lost that affected me so badly?

The loss of my perfect identity that I mentioned in chapter one still rumbled around at the root of everything. My idealised self-image had been in tatters for years now but the struggle to renew myself was not going well. Now, with this new upheaval in my life there seemed to be new layers of disappointments to deal with.

Coming to terms with the loss of my much loved home was a huge problem for me. That had been the anchor that had given me stability. I just loved that house in Edinburgh. It faced south and had windows the length of the walls and right down to the floor. The whole house was bathed in sunlight almost all day. It was modern, convenient, mine, and I loved it.

My habit of life had been lost. Having children meant that I knew the neighbours well and interacted on a daily basis with other parents, arranging babysitters, school runs, trips to the swimming pool and all the other minutiae of mothering. I picked the neighbourhood kids up from school. I child minded for friends to enable them to pursue their careers. The house became an after-school club most days. Chaos reigned as we all exchanged the days' adventures, baked pancakes, did homework and squabbled over trivia.

Regular contact with friends had been lost. My sister had lived across the road. My oldest friend was no more than a ten-minute drive away. I had a weekly schedule of meeting up with many of these friends and going to classes, playing badminton, meeting for coffee.

My job as a tour guide satisfied my love of the city and of history. I loved both the job and the tourists. It was time out, away from the house and family. It gave me self-worth and an expertise that was appreciated. I belonged there, in the city I was promoting, part of the fabric of it. Nothing gave me a buzz like the smell of diesel on a hot summer afternoon, forty tourists on an open-topped bus and a crowded Royal Mile. Happy faces, eager questions, cameras, accents, fun. That was living!

My life had been full and I had been content.

The last straw was the realisation that I had to leave our eldest daughter behind to complete her schooling in Edinburgh. She was to stay with dear family friends. For her it was an adventure. For me, it seemed like the end of life itself.

Loss. So much of that old life was the glue that held me together. I didn't realise how much I needed that glue until it all came unstuck and I fell to pieces. I was just like Humpty Dumpty. When poor Humpty had his great fall, all the King's horses and all the King's men couldn't put Humpty together again. When I had my great fall, I thought that I would be better off dead. Nothing could be done to put me together again. Nothing would ever be right again. Life, as I had known it, no longer existed. I was in exile. It seemed like the end of everything.

It seems we spend years working out what life is all about and how to tackle our lives to keep ourselves safe and happy. Then, hey presto, in the time it takes a bolt of lightening to zap the earth, all the certainties are gone and we are floundering in a world that seems to have changed overnight into a ghost ride in the fairground or the chamber of horrors at Madame Tussauds. For some, the bare-knuckle ride begins with redundancy. For others it may be illness. For still others it is bereavement. But for many, seemingly insignificant changes in their lives can trigger a disproportionate reaction, powerful enough to rocket them from happy, contented beings into trembling, fearful, confused searchers suddenly struggling through a life that seems to be out of their control. Often they are bemusedly asking, 'What happened? Where did all this come from?'

I now know that this is often a part of the normal pattern of life. Call it mid-life, call it a crisis of faith, call it what you like. It hurts. It's horrid. And I was hating every minute.

At some point in our lives we seem to lose all the certainties. Things go wrong. Life doesn't live up to our expectations. We have been flying through time and space quite contentedly. We crash. This was MY time, MY crash. Others have described the same phenomena, saints and sinners alike. Some have struggled and have eventually survived and grown stronger coming into a greater certainty of self and a new awareness of their spirituality. Some have been overwhelmed by the depth of the abandonment and have been apparently washed away. Many have wandered off to seek new paths, to follow other ideologies, to search on. All hearts yearn for something greater than themselves. Many only find the greater 'something' during their dark night of the soul. I think I truly found God in that time—not the 'idea' of God that I had carried around for years, but an awareness of something huge and powerful who could be found in the deepest part of my pain and who wanted to stick by me and help me through this rough patch.

Years later, when training in spirituality, I learned to ask a very important question. Where is God in all this? In the early stages of my life with depression I was asking a very different question. Why has God let me down? He didn't seem to be there at all. I was trying my best to follow him, do his will, to go where he sent me. And what was my reward for all this effort and struggle? An absent God, off on some other important business and leaving me to cope alone! Did he not care that I was crying myself to sleep? That I was unable to care for my children? That I couldn't even communicate with my husband?

It was going to take time for me to learn a new way of looking at things so that I could begin to see that, yes, God was there all right, even in the exile, but it seemed he was not to be found in the same places nor in the same guise. He had stopped treating me like a baby and was allowing me to take my first tottering steps in the big world. To let me practise my walking skills he had to stand back and watch me struggle for balance, sometimes falling down, sometimes catching on to the wrong aids, but slowly growing up into a big girl. It would take some time for me to realise that God was not a different being, but the father of a grown-up instead of the daddy of the child that I had been all these years. He was taking this opportunity, when I felt I had lost so much, to show me how little I needed. He was letting me grow up and develop new perspectives, shocking me into an uncomfortable period of growth—a steep, learning curve.

In the midst of this total experience of loss, it was necessary to lose one more thing; my inadequate ideas of God had to go so that I could discover the God who was adequate to meet me in my loss. Where was God in all this? He was right there where he always had been. But I wasn't recognising him.

This was something akin to 'the dark night of the soul' talked of by St John of the Cross. It was a period of deadness when it seemed God was absent from my world. He had been the air I breathed. I had fed on him, taken my energy and direction from him. If he had indeed gone from my world how could I live in this alien environment? I might as well try to breathe on the moon.

In the early stages, I thought I was being washed away. Not only was life overwhelmingly sad and difficult but also I really felt that God had left me. And for months I just had to hang on, searching, waiting, but most of the time just existing! It was a life of the living dead without any hope of a future or recovery. But, deep down, the process was working itself out and the foundations for recovery were being built, without my involvement or even my knowledge. While I was desperate for relief from my symptoms, the one who had created me in the first place was planning a radical makeover which would be a cure, not an just an aspirin for the soul. Things had to be dealt with! And one by one they all presented themselves for reappraisal.

For a start, I had to look again at my childhood concepts of God. I had got it wrong. Not totally wrong, perhaps. But I had built up an incomplete picture. I had grown into adulthood trailing behind me some very childish misconceptions, which were skewing my whole life stance.

Here are some memories of my childhood beliefs. How do they compare with yours?

First of all, God was good. Or so I was told. If I was good too then he would love me. If I was bad and didn't do the right things according to his book, then I would go to hell and be very unhappy. That, I think, is a fairly typical theology of the under sixteens, but I had never grown beyond that. I was working on the old principle that there was an unbreakable connection between sin and suffering, good works and happiness. If I had done well in school that day, I could tell my parents at dinner that night and they would be pleased. I might even get an extra helping of pudding because I had been such a good girl. If I had beaten up the girl from the tenement down the road, because she had called me names, then perhaps I wouldn't mention it. I knew better than ask for a telling off.

Secondly, God was a forgiving God—although I struggled to believe that. It was too good to be true! I wasn't seeing this forgiveness in adults.

My Dad used to pray with us every single night. Once we were tucked up in bed he would kneel down beside us and lead us in a prayer format that still seems a good one. He would start by thanking God for all the good things that had happened during the day and he would encourage us to join in with our highlights. Then he would pray for forgiveness for all our sins and again would ask us to list what they might be. Strangely enough, my sister and I became rather quiet at that point! Since we had little to say on that matter, he would confess what he imagined might have been our transgressions, ask for forgiveness and ask that we may be given the courage and ability to be better the next day. We then breathed a sigh of relief, knowing we were on the home straight, and plunged into a 'God bless' time when every nice person on the planet got an honourable mention along with the budgie and the neighbour's cat. Then we all said 'Amen' in a big, relieved voice.

My Dad was a loyal, dedicated Christian man and I have only the greatest of admiration for him. He loved me to bits, in his own way. He so much wanted me to share things with him and he would have prayed with me about all the little childish things, which were so important in my little life. He invited me to grow into a close, open relationship with him where we could have shared and learned together.

But I was born afraid! I was afraid to tell my Dad about myself and my worries, my fears and my failures—in case he wouldn't love me any more if he knew what I was really like. I knew nothing of a parent's love at that time. The kind of love that cannot give up, no matter what. The kind of love that would do anything to make it right for the child. The kind of love that would go on loving, even if the child was walking away in the other direction with nothing but contempt in his heart. That was the love my Dad had for me. And my dad was only human.

My heavenly dad has that kind of love for me too; only it can be multiplied by many millions. But when I was a child, I was scared of a God who was all powerful and demanded right living from his subjects. And I was scared that I would never be up to standard. So I did what I had taught myself to do in everyday life. I kept my head down and hoped that nobody, even God, would notice me.

Thirdly, I believed—without having to be taught—that I was born bad. I am not sure why I grew up believing that this was a fact. I am sure it would never be said to me. But somehow I grew up believing that I was so bad that I was unacceptable in God's eyes and in the eyes of most of the world. My mother is a perfectionist and tried everything to make her two daughters the best that they could be. She seemed to have more success with my sister, but I could only see the ways in which I didn't match up. My father was a stickler for obeying the rules and wanted us to follow his way as best we could. I was always a 'why' person and would only do things his way if I was sure there was good reason. I think I was a 'difficult' child!

Perhaps the religious fashion of the day played its part also. It was the early days of the Billy Graham crusades with all the pressures to turn away from your sin and give your heart to the Lord. Seen through my sensitive eyes this meant that if you didn't repent and turn to God then you were a bad person. I was too scared to go anywhere near God, therefore I was particularly bad! I chose to go to a Baptist Sunday School in those days, because it was much more fun than the Church of Scotland, but there also was the pressure to confess your sin in the hope that God would forgive all your past misdemeanours. I couldn't do it. It was far too scary!

In the fog of my depression I could sum up my theology of the moment with this; God was good; God was forgiving; but I had been such a bad person all my life that he had now, finally, abandoned me completely—and it was my own entire fault. There is nothing rational about depression! These obsessive thoughts clouded over my brain, squeezing out all the happiness and contentment I had previously enjoyed. I had been found out at last. I had been rumbled. Now my past was catching up with me. I deserved to be miserable.

My second-hand notions about the creator of the universe were completely out of touch with truth. They needed an overhaul and this was the time.

In my work with people I often come across mid-lifers. These are people who reach that awful stage of life when they have an unhappy epiphany. The realisation is that they have spent all these years doing things in a particular way, believing in certain defined principles, becoming a very defined person and in a moment of madness or misery, illness or 'ill-treatedness', tragedy or trauma, they sink to the bottom of the ocean and it seems that the bottom has fallen out of their lives. There is a horrid realisation that 'it hasn't worked', or 'it's not fair', or 'I have been so stupid!' They have tried so hard to do things the right way and somehow it hasn't worked out, life has become topsy-turvy and they cannot see a way ahead.

That is the moment I encourage these people to sit at the bottom of the sea or the mountain or the wall and do a spot of reconsidering. And three things need to be looked at;

> our view of ourselves (self-awareness)
> our way of looking at the world (world view)
> and what we think God is like (view of God)

We just can't get through that difficult mid-life time without doing the work, chucking away many out-dated views and beginning again on a new and stronger foundation.

We never emerge from that mid-life phase the same as we went into it. We are like caterpillars entering a cocoon and allowing the magic of nature to take its course before slowly unveiling the beauty of the new butterfly. Basically it has the same DNA but it now has shape and form and definition and a beauty altogether lacking in its early days. We can emerge also and know that we never want to go back to the days of eating cabbage leaves!

Loss—some things are better lost!

To ponder:

We all have views on many things.

Let us look at the way:

      we see THE WORLD

      we look at GOD and

      we understand OURSELVES.

These three are inter-related. Each one is dependent of the others. Change the way we understand any one of these and our lives change. Sometimes subtly and occasionally they change in ways that alter our lives.

Try the following exercise:

Decide which of the trio you want to look at first. Prepare to make lists.

      1. List 5 positive ways in which you understand the world/God/yourself.

      2. Then list 5 negative ways in which you see the world/God/yourself.

      3. Consider each of these things in turn and ask yourself where each idea came from.

For instance, my grandfather was wheelchair-bound, a tyrant of a boss but very fond of me as his grandchild. He allowed me to sit on his knee as he roamed around the garage where he worked and I

was so aware of him being critical and demanding of his employees. But he was never anything but kind to me, his beloved child. Did this help to paint my picture of God? Can you think back? Just allow your mind to wander and remember long-forgotten snippets of these early days. Don't rush this, you may want to write in your journal or scribble sketches or talk to someone who knows you well.

4. Look again at your list. Ask yourself if you believe your assertion to be true, false or if you don't know. Against each of your answers write T for true, F for false or DK for don't know.

5. Give yourself pondering time and note your thoughts and observations over the days.

6. Then do the same with the other two in the trio.

Chapter 3

The Great Depression

'I am NOT depressed.' I sounded a note of desperation as I argued with my GP. 'I don't care what is wrong with me but I WILL NOT be depressed!'

She gave me a long, measuring look, concentrated again on her notes and then said, 'There's nothing wrong with being depressed, you know. It's just an illness. Some people need an inhaler to relieve their asthma. Or maybe they have a thyroid problem and they need extra thyroxin to help them keep alive. I will give you anti-depressants and I guarantee that you will feel much more like yourself again in just a few weeks.'

I could not and would not do that. I WAS NOT having anti-depressants. What normal person with a normal life needed to live on Prozac? I was NOT depressed. OK, I was a bit bad-tempered and a bit unhappy. I shouted a lot and cried a bit and I was just so tired all the time. And I hated going out and facing people. And maybe I was just a tiny bit paranoid about all the bad things that were surely going to happen any day now. But I was NOT depressed. That was a ridiculous idea. What kind of doctor did she think she was?

I went home that day in a rage and cleaned the kitchen. I clattered around, throwing things in cupboards, scrubbing worktops, mopping the floors. And through gritted teeth I kept repeating things like, 'Stupid woman! What makes her think I'm depressed? And how dare she! There's nothing wrong with me!'

An hour later and I was mopping the floor with my tears. I had slipped on the wet surface, fallen heavily and ended in a heap, whimpering for half an hour. Then my duvet claimed me for the next three days where I had plenty time to cry over the diagnosis of depression. 'How dare that woman tell me I'm depressed,' turned to 'I am so ashamed of myself. How can I let myself get into this state? I will have to try harder.'

And so I did. The worse I got, the harder I tried to solve my problems. I worked very hard at being 'normal' but everything I did only worked for five minutes because I lacked the skills I needed in this deep water. I had never had to swim in this kind of whirlpool before and I didn't have the strength or the skill to keep afloat. I was in over my head. I was drowning. But the rescue boat had 'anti-depressant' plastered on the side of it. So I let it go by. Because, after all, I wasn't depressed!

For five stupid years I fought off the diagnosis. In that time I became a bit of an amateur expert in two things. I allowed my poor doctor to consider hormone trouble as a possible cause for my problems. So I tried the lot and got to know my subject fairly well. And when that failed and she was ready to either kill herself or kill me, she suggested I tried homeopathic medicine. That was fascinating and I enjoyed playing with the whole subject of how—and even if—any of it worked. It amused me for a time. But none of it made me any better.

And so eventually, when I was at the end of my rope and the doctor had decided to retire—no, the two were NOT connected (I don't think!)—I tearfully agreed to try the dreaded Prozac for a couple of months. I told no one except my husband. He was sworn to secrecy. I couldn't have anyone knowing that I was such a poor wreck that I needed to stoop that low. I cried every morning as I secretly reached for the pills, hating myself for my weakness in needing them. And still I hid behind locked doors, hiding myself from a world that was too bright, too loud, and too happy. A world I thought I could never re-enter.

It took five weeks. A normal Friday morning saw me scuttle to my car, rattle round the supermarket and beetle off home again without talking to anyone and without a glance around me at the scary people who might be there. This particular morning I was driving out of the car park, groceries neatly packed in the boot, and I heard a wee voice in my head say, 'What a gorgeous morning. It seems a shame to go home so soon. Let's go the library.'

Where did that come from? I don't go gallivanting around. I need to get home. I need to get inside my house, lock the door and be alone. But the voice was adamant. I could go to the library. Why not? I used to do that. I used to enjoy doing that.

And so I went to the library. I had a nice time there and the journey home seemed brighter, the sun warmer, my heart softer. If this was Prozac, then it should be in the water supply. We should all have this. Everybody should feel as good as I did at that moment. I had taken the first step towards health.

I know now that anti-depressants on their own don't work to cure depression. But without them I would never have had the strength, energy or clarity to do the inner work needed to begin to live a healthy and happy life. They were the crutch I needed for a time to hold me up while I mended all the broken bits. And there were lots of broken or badly built bits of my psyche that needed attention. And that was to be the next step towards wholeness.

The first of the 'botched jobs' to be reworked was my attitude towards emotion. When I was suffering so badly with depression I was awash with unexplained emotion, which seemed to swish around and would have drowned me if I didn't get rid of it quickly. So rather than deal with emotion, I tended to disregard it. Ignore it and it will go away, was my naïve and misguided theory.

But in ignoring emotion I had made a huge mistake. This was to be the biggest discovery for my eventual recovery. Emotion MUST be dealt with. If it is recognised and used appropriately we can move on unencumbered. If we don't allow ourselves to feel the emotion when it strikes, we can't deal with it. So it goes into a big pot inside us. The big pot gets over-filled. The lid won't go on. We have to sit on the lid to keep all the emotion out of sight. We get exhausted. The emotion all spills out in a huge mess. We get overwhelmed. We drown in all the gunge! That's depression!

My fear of emotion came from my parents. Previous generations were scared of emotions and disregarded them, feeling they were not only unnecessary but a hindrance to us. The motto was to ignore how we feel and just get on with life. It's a bit like saying ignore the state of your engine and just drive! It is a ridiculous theory, and has served us all badly.

My emotional intelligence had suffered from neglect over many years. For as long as I could remember I had been moody but I could never work out why I swept from high good humour to feeling worthless and sad in a fraction of a second. There seemed no reason for these mood swings so I assumed over the years that this was a quirk in my personality and that was just the way it was. It was a structural fault in my psyche. So, in a way, the moodiness defined me. That's the way it was. I couldn't help it.

In my childhood home anger was never expressed. It was there alright—in bucketfuls. But it was kept hidden beneath my mother's iron control. So I had grown up thinking anger was bad, harmful and that nice people didn't do that kind of thing. On the odd occasion when anger had burst out of me I was punished—by my very angry mother. And yet, I remember how good it felt, just for a second, to rant and shout and enjoy the release of the rage.

In depression, the mood swings were more intense and the worthless, sad moments threatened to drown me. The anger, never acknowledged, was a frozen lump deep inside, seeming to have nothing to do with my mood. Once the anti-depressants took effect and I once again began to feel something akin to happiness, I looked more closely at the changes in mood that I experienced. They seemed less random when examined under a microscope, and almost always had a trigger point.

Let me tell you of one such incident.

I had been in business for a year, I was life coaching—using my new qualifications as a spiritual director—and teaching the Enneagram system of personality analysis. The first nine months were great because I had so many ideas and projects and my creative juices were flowing abundantly. I loved my teaching and got such a buzz from seeing people's lives changed as they recognised themselves in the Enneagram system. In my Spiritual Direction work I had a few clients who came monthly to share their journeys with me and sometimes I was able to help them find the way ahead. I was learning so much and feeling energised to know that I had a 'calling' and I loved the work.

Christmas came and went. The New Year arrived and, with it, all my resolutions to work harder, be a success, be myself and be a star. The depression was behind me. I felt that I had arrived! I was fulfilled and confident and I could really do this well. I was so much looking forward to restarting work at the end of the holidays.

But within days, I was at the bottom of the tank, and I felt as though I was drowning. I felt worthless, weepy, a total failure and with no shred of ability to do anything with my life. I had been a terrible mother; a hopeless wife and (unsurprisingly in my eyes!) nobody liked me. I was, and felt I had always been, a failure.

It took some time before I asked myself what had taken me from a state of contentment and fulfilment to this dark hole of misery. Why had my mind been chirping, 'I can do this! I can do this!' and suddenly changed its tune to 'I can't do it! I know I just can't do it! And I need to go to bed.'

At first I sat in my misery with no answers, just the sick feeling that I was in that place of despair yet again. I had thought I was better at life now and could live on a high all the time. What had happened to me? Slowly and gradually, I found the trigger and began to piece together the jigsaw.

During the holiday time we had been at a party where we met old friends who were dear to us still, although our paths crossed less often. We had a lovely evening with them all. And so it was with real pleasure that I answered the phone two days later and said 'I'd love to,' when Monica invited me out for lunch. The lunch didn't go too well, actually, but I thought it was probably my fault since I ran out of conversation very quickly and Monica didn't seem to have much to say. I wondered afterwards why she had invited me at all because she seemed a bit irritated all the time we were eating. But I went home, put it all out of my mind and got on with life.

Days later, huddled up, distressed and sorry for myself, I thought back to our time together and it struck me, out of the blue, that Monica had been angry with me. I hate anyone being angry with me. It makes me feel a failure, unlovable and worth nothing and it takes me right back to when I was a little girl realising that adults around me were angry with me again. And since I often didn't know why they were angry with me, I assumed it was because I wasn't a very nice person and they didn't love me. I just got out of the way, tried to keep my head down and hoped I would become invisible.

So instead of standing up for myself with Monica, I reacted as I had done when I was a child. I pushed the emotions away out of sight and denied that anything unpleasant had happened. That had been my way of coping with anger when I was six years old and I responded again in the same way, out of habit. Monica was angry with me because my lifestyle didn't meet with her approval. I wasn't supporting my husband as she felt I should be and there were things that I had allowed to slip from my life; things which seemed very important to her. I was not living up to her standards and she took it upon herself to remonstrate with me.

I didn't take time to argue with her or even discuss what she thought was the problem. I just reacted by withdrawing myself from her company, tried to think no more about it all and went home, hoping I wouldn't have to see Monica for a very long time!

But three days later, I was in bed, sluggish, unwell and with not an ounce of self-esteem. And the trigger to this entire thing happening was back there in the restaurant when Monica showed me her disapproval.

With today's wisdom I would have dealt with that incident very differently. On seeing my mood plunge down to sadness, I should have asked myself immediately what had caused the change. I could have traced back the change of mood to my lunch with Monica.

Then I would have looked at the emotion the incident had brought out.

The conversation had made me feel sad because I sensed her disapproval.

It made me anxious and fearful because I had lost her approval and regard. I felt as though she no longer liked me. She thought I was wrong in my new lifestyle. And, needing the approval of others, I felt worthless.

It made me feel discouraged. I had climbed a long, steep path from the early days of depression; I had turned my life around and was starting along the new road of self-employment in spiritual direction and life coaching. I had thought I was doing ok.

The next stage of unpacking my descent into the abyss would have been to listen to my thoughts—so often disregarded.

I was thinking, 'I am useless. I've always been useless. How stupid to believe that my life was actually going anywhere. I will never be any good. I try so hard but I never win. I will always be a hopeless person. I don't know why I even try any more.'

Listen to yourself when you're depressed. None of that is true! The incident with Monica made me think these things **were** true. But by laying out my emotions and my negative thoughts, I could see and hear how stupid it all was.

And then came the anger. I always prided myself on the fact that I didn't DO anger. I was calm and peaceful and accepting. I didn't need to be angry.

Yes, I WAS arrogant—and a liar. We all DO anger. And if we don't then we should.

In recognising the emotions and the thoughts connected to my lunchtime date with Monica, I allowed myself to become angry with HER instead of being angry with ME—much healthier. I WAS angry and I needed to allow myself to feel it and then I could move on and leave the incident—and the resulting depression—behind me.

She had no right to criticise my line of work or my lifestyle just because it was different from her chosen path and her ideals. This was MY life, MY path, MY journey. It was MY choice, MY responsibility. It had nothing at all to do with her.

I was out of the pit! I was free! In allowing myself to feel the emotion—in this case, anger—I was able to move through it to a place of peace and assurance. This system of looking at the trigger, the emotions and the thoughts actually worked.

And that has been the system that works for me every time. I can unpack it all in just a few seconds now. And in recognising and dealing with emotion immediately I am no longer run by this dark, unrecognised undercurrent that kept sweeping me off course and into deep water. With this system in place, I am learning to swim.

One of the most important tools had been discovered. I was learning to recognise and deal with my emotions.

To ponder:

People who are depressed feel like they're drowning. The water is over their heads and they don't know how to swim. They try hard in their panic. They really are fighting for life. But their efforts are unproductive because they don't have the skills they need to support themselves under water. They will die if they stop trying. But they will die if they continue trying. They will tire and sink into the great abyss.

Better by far to let the water support them, than to fight the water and lose the battle.

If you are depressed there are techniques to learn to help you swim in this deadly water you are currently experiencing.

1. Are there regrets, guilty thoughts, memories that haunt you? Can you begin to identify some of them and write them down? It is sufficient to remember and name them for now.

2. Can you list the emotions you feel? Like Rumplestiltskin[1] found—to name your emotions as

---

[1] Remember the fairy story of Rumplestiltskin—as soon as he was named he lost his power. So it will be with you.

they invade your space means they will lose some of their power.

3. Watch as the tide washes in concerns that are not yours but which you feel deeply. An accident in the street, something on the news, a story you hear in conversation. Some of these things can draw you down into the abyss of sadness. Yet many of these occurrences are NOT yours to worry about. A quick prayer to the God who CAN do something about them is better that you taking on all the worry and concern. Don't let these things pull you down beneath the waves. Build boundaries to keep the tidal wave at bay.

4. Can you name some of these circumstances? List the concerns of others or of the wider world that pull you down into worry and sadness and bleakness.

Chapter 4
Staying out of jail

If you want to stay out of real prison; you have to obey the law of the land. To stay out of the prison of depression, then there are a whole set of laws that must be obeyed. But they are not written down anywhere. You can't buy a highway code for depression. No manufacturer's instructions come with the umbilical cord. It seems to be a case of trial and error. We need to experience the error before the trial is over and we walk lightly across the earth.

If the manual existed it would have a vast section on dealing with emotions. There are actually only four emotions. Anger, fear, joy and sadness. And yet we use hundreds of words to describe how we feel. I use polite words to describe my anger; frustrated, cross, irritated, and ruffled. For fear—because I am usually trying to be brave—I will say I am a little anxious or that I am troubled by something. For joy—why won't I allow myself to feel joy?—I will use words like content or peaceful. And for sadness—well, I try not to feel sad and refusing to speak about the sadness was my way of dealing with it for many years.

That had to change. Rule 1 in the invisible manual of instructions for healthy living—understand, feel and learn to embrace emotions. Better to feel them, deal with them and get them out the way than to fill up the pot to bursting point and watch it all explode in a huge volcanic eruption. Very messy! Not a pretty sight.

A huge part of depression grows out of our tangle of emotions and our inexperience in dealing with them. If we don't feel emotions it's because we are using huge amounts of energy to keep them out of our awareness. This is unhealthy and must be tackled if we are to become well and remain healthy and whole.

For years and years—probably since I was four years old—I had avoided feeling any emotion. It was as if I had a huge pot inside me and every time an emotion came into sight, I would drop it into the pot and put the lid down very firmly on top of it. After a while the pot got pretty full but I could still stuff these emotions into it. By the time I got depressed I had to sit on the pot in order to keep the lid on. But I was doing it, using lots of effort, but succeeding in keeping all emotion firmly out of sight and faking happiness whenever I could. It was more comfortable to feel nothing than risk feeling uncomfortable.

Depressives hardly feel any emotion, other than sadness. We seem to have developed a special talent for stuffing all the goodness of emotion into the deepest pit and only allowing sadness to escape. Most of the time we even keep that to a minimum and aim for emptiness because it is less painful than sadness. We work on everything being grey and neutral.

In depression, even beauty is banned from our awareness. It brings dangerous colour to the grey and sits in stark contrast to the sadness, making us confused and opening us to the possibility of even more emotion. Beauty in nature, for example, would normally leave us feeling, 'WOW!' with a sneaking feeling of joy crossing our awareness. Seeing pretty things on a shopping spree infuses us with happiness or maybe envy or even sadness if we know we would never be able to own that or wear that.

And the emotion would then open up the guilt. Then we would feel REALLY bad, because guilt must be one of the very worst of feelings. We don't want to deal with that. We don't have the energy to deal with any of it. So we don't go there. We stay in the grey place and accept it as it is; the best there is available. No highs, no lows, just emptiness. We can live with that. We've got used to it.

Guilt—have we any idea what we feel guilty about? Often we who are depressed feel a blanket guilt—nothing specific—just vague feelings that we have said something, done something, been bad, or transgressed in some unknown way. The depressive is full of guilt about feelings, desires and impulses he's not even aware he has. We MUST be guilty of something because that's how it feels. That is part of depression. It is probably not the truth but it sure feels true to us.

The truth is that it is likely that we HAVE transgressed in some way. Everybody does. But the truth also is that we are no worse than anyone else and God is willing to forgive the sin of the depressed person as readily as that of the healthy sinner. Let us rest in that knowledge.

If we know what our emotions are we will be better placed to recognise why we feel guilty. If we are going to feel guilty anyway, we are as well to understand what the guilt is about. It's an unfair world! We don't get to feel the emotions—good or bad—but we still get to feel guilty about them anyway. This only makes us more depressed. If we are going to feel the guilt and the associated change in mood, wouldn't we be better to know what the emotions were all about? Maybe we could even enjoy them!

To encourage you to do this exercise let me tell you the story of Amy. Amy had been traumatised by a violent sexual attack when only twelve. She had been unable to deal with it at such a young age and it wasn't until years later that she sought help. By then the situation was very hard to untangle and she was a deeply unhappy girl.

During counselling she was encouraged to re-enter the morass of emotion that she had stuffed into the big pot inside herself for so long. What a painful, bleak few months for her, trawling through the anger, the shame, the guilt. She experienced anew so much deeply buried raw emotion and began to enter into a previously unknown and unacknowledged rage that seemed to consume her for several weeks. She wondered if she would ever come to the end of this whirlwind of horror and despair she had entered into.

But then Amy's birthday weekend came around and a good friend decided to make it one to remember. Amy dreaded it, feeling too tired to fake the happiness expected of her. But much to her surprise and delight, Amy had a wonderful weekend when she was able to experience pleasure and enjoy fun for the first time in years.

Having allowed herself to experience the horror and bleakness of past emotions, Amy had been out of jail for that wonderful birthday weekend. Acknowledging past hurt, sadness, fear and anger, she was able also to enter into a place of joy. She had been unable to enjoy herself for years.

Amy's story touched me deeply. Journeying with her was a great privilege and a great distress all at once. It made me cry. It made me rage. It made me so angry that her abuser was still out there. I felt impotent with fury that she was so damaged by that man and he would never know her pain, never understand what he had done to her. I hated him so violently that I wanted to go out there, private eye extraordinaire, find him, tie him up, beat him senseless and drag him in to the nearest police station.

In allowing myself to become so involved in the pain of another person, I was doing a disservice to both Amy and to myself. This had become a pattern in my life. Because I love to listen to people's stories and help them through painful situations, it is only natural and right that I enter into their feelings and feel their pain. But my big failing here was that I had no boundaries. I was useless to Amy because all her pain had cascaded over into my life and I was drowning in it. I cried as I sat with her. I imagined how I would feel if it had happened to me. The sadness seeped into me like autumn damp into fallen leaves. I was left a soggy mess of tears every time I saw her.

And there were others. I felt everyone's pain so deeply. Even more damaging was that I wouldn't walk away from the pain and live a normal life. I felt that in doing so I would be letting the people down. By me being as upset as they were, I felt that I was helping them. This was skewed thinking. What actually happened was that the person in question would get on with life very competently with or without my involvement and I would be imprisoned in their mess and in their emotion so completely that I had no life of my own. It became like physical pain for me. And if I enjoyed my own life in the meantime, I would feel so guilty.

I had never heard of boundaries.

Today I walked the coastal path between two of our East Neuk villages. It was a beautiful spring day; fresh, brisk and blustery, the sun warm and bright and the tide running high—very high. At one point it had run right up the beach and the dunes were being swamped by the incoming waves. A few yards further up and golfers were poised on the green ready to putt, unaware of the rising tide creeping closer and closer. Further round the coast at Anstruther the spring tide had silently climbed on to the road, swamping the harbour car park and even flooding the shops on the other side of the road. Some tides are dangerously high, a threat to all of us living close to the sea.

Without boundaries—sea walls and protective barriers—Scotland would be at risk of shrinking as high tides sweep around the coast twice every day. We need to look after our towns and villages, making sure they are safe from the power of the elements.

And in the same way our emotions batter down our small resistance and force us to be submerged in the flood. And so we sink in the waves. We are lost in the strong currents. We are washed away by the power of the feelings that we feel so deeply and cannot ignore. This is not good for any of us. But for the depressed person it is a force imposed upon us that we just can't handle.

But whether or not we have learned to build boundaries, we have to at least recognise and deal with the emotions that all too readily flood over us and leave us gasping for breath. When things happen that upset or disturb us, and change the mood of our day, don't kick the cat or throw the frying pan across the room. Ask yourself a few questions and tease out your reaction.

- First of all, what happened? Something did. If your mood suddenly changes then it is always caused by something. It may be an event. Or a memory. Or somebody's reaction. Or a face that reminds you of someone or of a past sadness. Find the trigger for the change. There WILL be a trigger. Sometimes you have to really go back over the last hours to find it. But it is essential to the exercise that you know what has plunged you into a dark mood.

- Next, ask yourself, 'How do I feel right now?' There are four categories of feelings. They are;

fear
sadness
joy
anger

There are, of course, many adjectives within these broad categories. Try to identify how you feel. Which of the following words best describes the way you feel right now? If none of these words is suitable, write down your own—but only use one word.

determined
sorrowful
distressed withdrawn
thankful scared tired
worried moody energized
gutted perplexed agitated
glad cautious excited
great uncertain delirious
sad alive mad cast-down
cross euphoric panicky
worn-out discouraged sick
frustrated
content weepy shocked
peaceful anxious
disappointed

• Once you have identified the emotion of the moment, let us move onto the thoughts that churn around in your head. What is YOUR tape? Mine is 'I'm hopeless' or 'I'll never be any good' or 'I try so hard but never get it right'. Notice your own inner chant. And write these thoughts in your journal.

• Then imagine. A dear friend comes to you with this scenario and asks your advice. What would you say to them? What would you advise? I guess you would try hard to be understanding, to be kind and to encourage your friend. You would look for the positives and try to steer them away from the negative viewpoint.

• Then, listen to yourself. Try to do the same to yourself. Be understanding. Be kind. Look at the positives.

Writing all this down helps. Get yourself a notebook. You will need it, because these things happen all the time. Every day we have a change of mood, maybe several times a day. And catching the emotions as they are happening will be a great tool to use. But if you don't write it down, you will soon forget and have to learn the lessons all over again the next time.

When suffering from depression—and even sometimes when you aren't—you will have days when you just can't get up and face the day. Sadness is the mood of that day and it saps all the energy out of you and you just can't face it. It is all too much of an effort. You are too tired. You don't have the energy to do whatever the day promises. Or you are looking at the long hours of a free day and you can't face it.

For days like this you need different tools.

A magic wand would be good. One that would transform you into a fully dressed and functioning person in the blink of an eye. I can't offer one of those. But what I have, I offer you here.

I know from long experience that if I lie in bed all day I will feel worse. Much worse! So I have to gently coax myself on, the way I would do with a child. I wake up needing a cup of tea. Eventually, I will drag myself up to put the kettle on. At that moment I have to go into coaxing mode. I say to myself, 'You would feel better if you just put the washing on while you are downstairs anyway.' I do it carelessly but quickly then drag myself back to bed. I know I will feel better if I clean my teeth. While in the bathroom I force myself to spray some cleaning liquid into the wash basin. Then I crawl back to bed. An hour later, I really need to go to the loo. So I wipe and rinse the basin before I go back to bed. I can coax myself through a few hours in this way. Eventually I will sleep again, probably for hours.

Then on waking well into the day, I can review the day. Yes, I caught up on sleep and rest. Yes, I hid from the world and its expectations of me. Yes, I had the duvet day. But, you know what? I cleaned the washbasin and I did a washing. Maybe before I make some toast and more tea, maybe I will just hang up the washing, and if I have the energy I could clear away all the shampoo bottles lying around the bathroom. Maybe tidy up a bit. Gosh, I've had a productive day!

Then there are the other days, better than duvet days, but days when you just can't get started. You are up and dressed and wonder what more the world expects of you. It was hard enough to get that far. My temptation at that point is to sit down with a cup of tea and a magazine. Again I try to go into coaxing mode. I put the kettle on and find one very small thing that I might do before I make my tea. It's what I call a 'just do and then' day. I will just wipe the crumbs off the worktop and then I will sit down with my tea. After I've done that I look for another tiny thing I might do before I sit down again. It's a game I play. And it becomes fun. How many tiny little jobs can I squeeze in before I drink this long-promised cup of tea? Occasionally I get so carried away that I reach lunchtime without the sustenance that I promised myself hours before. Most days I get a few jobs done, feel my self-esteem rise a little and then enjoy the tea and the magazine.

It's got a lot to do with being in control of something, however small, in your life. A depressed person has lost control of so many areas of life. It's hard to see how to get that control back so that you can feel better about yourself. It can't be done in one go. But it is a problem that you can eat into little bit by little bit. It might be useful to write a list of little things that, if done, would make an enormous difference to the way you feel. It might be tidying your desk or your pan drawer or your bedside table. It might be making a phone call or writing a letter. It could be paying a bill that is worrying you, or speaking to your bank about changing an account. Beside each item, write the length of time the task would probably take. Then when you are ready—or maybe even if you're not ready but willing to try— choose one of the tasks that would take a short amount of time and just do it. 'Just do it!' should become one of your mantras. Don't think about it. Just do it.

Once the list is made, check it regularly so that you begin to know it off by heart. And tick off the items as you go along. What a great feeling it is to put a line through each task. Done! I did that! I can do it! I am re-gaining control, little by little.

Whew! If you are a depressed person you will feel exhausted just reading the last page, never mind taking the advice and getting started. The best advice I can give you here is to treat yourself like a child for a while. Love yourself as you would love the child. Be gentle on yourself but also be firm. Many a child grows up defeated because of a harsh parent. But a child can also grow up spoilt and wasted by a parent who has been too soft. Take the middle road here. Treat yourself with respect; be gentle when that is what you need, but also be firm with yourself. Don't allow destructive behaviours like sleeping all day or drinking to blot out the pain and let personal hygiene go. A good parent would encourage, be gentle but also insist that you love yourself enough to do at least the minimum towards recovery.

And so—some more tools for the journey. Dealing with your emotions and treating yourself gently. This is hard work but the tools all help.

To ponder:

A mood change will ALWAYS be triggered by something. It might be an actual incident or a memory, a snatch of music, a smell, or even just noticing something small and beautiful.

Do the following exercise several times a day.

Stop. Close your eyes. Ask yourself, "What emotions am I feeling right now?" Look back a few pages to the list of emotions if you need help. Write down the emotion. Just begin to notice your emotions as they move and flow throughout the day.

And then, at night, write a few lines about what made you feel this way.

Ask yourself if something happened to make you feel like this. Write down the triggers. Allow yourself some time to live with the feelings this brings up.

Emotion is never WRONG. Emotion JUST IS. Feel it and move on from it. Don't be afraid of it. It is a natural part of life to feel them. Relax!

Chapter 5
Self-awareness

Sometimes you fall into life-changing situations without even noticing.

'Welcome to the course.' The speaker was frighteningly efficient, glancing round the room and looking right into our souls. 'Let's take time to introduce ourselves and perhaps each of you might tell us what attracted you to this weekend's subject matter.'

Nothing had attracted me at all. What's more, it was a weekend which should have been time off and I was wishing I had stayed at home! But, since that would have sounded rather impolite, I thought I had better spin a more positive tale. The truth was that my boss had suggested that two members of staff registered for the course and then go home and teach it to the rest of our staff community of about eighteen members. We all lived and worked together, many even sharing houses, and we functioned like a family unit, albeit a slightly dysfunctional one. We needed the insights that this course had to offer. But I was extremely fearful of the subject matter and hoped that if I sat very quietly I might become invisible.

I am tall, wear a fairly confident mask and have the unfortunate compulsion to talk to everybody. Therefore, people tend to think—quite wrongly, as it happens—that I am confident and able, and can be used to initiate sensitive conversations. So the speaker turned to me and said,

'We'll start with you, Dorothy. Why are you here this weekend?'

Realising too late that I had not, in fact, become invisible, I opened my mouth and tried to sound intelligent. But I fooled no one, stuttering as I tried to pronounce the name of the course and blushing with shame as I tried to give a creditable reason for perhaps wanting to be there. I told the truth however, about taking the course back to Crieff and helping to sort out staffing problems. But that proved to be a mistake.

'My dear,' answered our course leader, 'You are on an Enneagram course. The Enneagram is a personality profiling system and a tool for self-development. I stress that it is for SELF-development, not that of your staff. I give you permission to pack your bags right now and go home if you are not prepared to work on your OWN personality over the next forty-eight hours.'

Still living in the twilight days of depression, I took this badly, unable to bear the humiliation that I felt at this scolding. But nor did I have the courage to go and pack my bags, although I had to hold myself down in the chair! The only thing I really wanted to do was run. I was quite unprepared for this kind of forthrightness and even less prepared to have my personality analysed and judged and no doubt found to be severely wanting. My heart was pounding; I broke out in a sweat and fought to hold back the tears. But I stayed in my seat, only just!

Everyone else was on a mission to reform themselves! I marvelled at them. If there was something to reform, then they must have a personality to work on. I wasn't at all sure that I had a personality in any shape or form so the first task was to find one. And thankfully that seemed to be the aim of the first twenty-four hours. That, however, proved harder than it sounded. We weren't allowed to invent a personality. We had actually to get in touch with our own, by peeling back the layers and finding the gem of our essence at the centre of our being.

I was unaware of anything at my centre. I had worn a mask for years. In fact, I had a cupboard full of them and carefully picked one out each day to suit the occasion. I had a 'walking the dog' mask, which I kept with my fleecy jacket, wellies and the dog's lead. It showed an energetic forty year old with a busy day ahead and purpose in her soul. Then there was a 'going out for coffee' mask, which belonged to a sophisticated, well-dressed suburban housewife. In the afternoon I wore the 'dedicated mother' mask while I stood at the school gate. For my job as a tour guide I would choose the 'all-knowing, all-seeing, singing, dancing, Harry Lauder, 'och aye the noo' mask which came in seven varieties of tartan. There was a mask for visits to the parents, another for church. And a very carefully moulded one for office occasions with my husband. Each painted one or other aspect of the person I had thought I was.

On that evening I was being asked to strip away all these masks and look at the real me, the one I had tried to ignore for forty years, the one who lived in the cupboard with the masks but was never allowed out. The one I no longer recognised.

Do we all wear masks, I wonder? A face for each situation, a careful blend of what is expected of us and what we feel inclined to reveal? I had never thought about it before, preferring to play my various parts in life's drama and try to stuff down any emotion I might feel which would spoil the act. Because—why? Probably because I was afraid. What if I revealed the real me, supposing I knew where to look for it, and nobody liked it? What if my husband had married the 'flirtatious blond with long legs' mask and then found out that there was someone else hiding behind it? He might not like the other one, the real me. And just as worrying was the fear that perhaps there was nothing at all behind the series of elaborate masks. Not only was I invisible, but I didn't exist at all.

The Enneagram system teaches that there are basically nine personality types, within which each of us is unique. We all have our gifts and our challenges, our pitfalls, our endearing qualities and a favourite way of reacting to the world. Now that I am actually teaching the system myself I find it endlessly exciting to draw out all the strands of a personality and see the unique twist each of us has inherited from our Heavenly Father. There are endless combinations of gifts, quirks and attitudes, all pulled together into any one of us, making each of us exciting, vibrant individuals. God made us all different. But he DID make us, and we are not here in our skins by accident. We are each lovingly hand-crafted and sculptured to be the way we are. And far from appreciating that, I was busy hiding myself away so that nobody would know the real me.

It took the whole of that weekend for me to recognise myself in any of the nine categories of the

Enneagram system. Others were storming ahead of me, finding their type within hours and going on to celebrate how special they were with all their gifts and abilities. Hardly had they had time to rest on their laurels when they were off again, noticing their perpetual bad habits and confessing their habitual sins. Then they were racing along the highway of reinventing themselves into new super-duper models of the same type but with all their wrinkles ironed out. And then, complete with a botoxed soul and sparkling personality, they launched into the next phase of their lives with vitality and energy that would spark fear into the Dalai Lama himself! It was exhausting to watch.

They all seemed so self-aware! Why could I only crawl at a snail's pace behind them? I was poking my antenna out trying to make sense of the way ahead, but more often than not, withdrawing into my shell and becoming invisible again. I didn't seem to have the strength or energy to tackle the process in one go.

By the Sunday afternoon I was beginning to get a clearer picture. I realised that very little of my behaviour pointed to the real 'me'. My behaviour was dependant on the mask I wore. Rather it was the motivation behind my behaviour that would be the important thing to recognise in deciphering my personality. Little by little, I drew out strands of character, plucking them from the inner darkness, and stacking them up, the better to study them.

Strand number one. I was, and am still, motivated by a need to be at peace with people and with God. Then add to that my equal desire to be at peace with my children, my husband, the neighbours, my colleagues, the bus driver, the cashier at the supermarket, my parents, my bosses, my cleaning lady, the postman, the bank manager, the Prime Minister and the lollipop lady—and perhaps you can see why I needed all these masks. And could this help to explain why I was suffering from depression? What I surely was suffering from was an impossible ideal that was as unrealistic as it was damaging. I could never please everybody all the time! And what about myself? Did I ever consider what I wanted or was the whole point of my existence to fit in with the rest of the world? No wonder I had felt that I was a non-person. If I had ever had a personality at all, I was fast torpedoing the last shreds of it out of existence.

But in recognising that, I had made a big breakthrough in my search for the non-person hiding in the inner darkness. What else lay hidden in there? This was becoming quite exciting after all!

Strand number two. I had to admit to the humiliation of having low self-esteem. I began to realise why my friends teased me about constantly apologising for myself. I had thought of that particular quality as humility, a worthy enough quality in itself, but perhaps the word 'sorry' was used too regularly in my vocabulary. Generally speaking, it was quite possible, and even likely, that whatever situation had gone wrong could well have been my fault. Being brought up by a perfectionist, I usually found myself in the wrong. It seemed easier to apologise first and think about it later, if really necessary.

If I had friends in for dinner and the veggies were overdone, I would apologise immediately, before they could discover the truth for themselves. If someone admired my hand knitted Aran jersey, I would point out to them that I had made a mistake in the pattern just here on the sleeve. When, from time to time, my husband would comment on how nice I looked, I would demur and blame the new shirt I was wearing, almost apologising for daring to be a pleasing sight. I was good at apologising. I had turned it into an art form.

But the Enneagram system was able to take these smallest of insights and make sense of them. Our course leader and resident expert, was able to prod a little, ask a few penetrating questions, which were very hard to answer, and hey presto, I discovered that I wasn't a non-person at all. I really did exist and I was an Enneagram number NINE type personality, a peacemaker. Hurrah! I had a personality! Where had it come from? Had it always been lurking in there, hiding in the mists of my foggy brain, with too little self-esteem to let its face be seen, even by me? Yes, I think it has always been there. But I had to follow a trail of crumbs back to the gingerbread house of childhood before I could begin to understand.

Little Dotty was an insecure baby. She cried when she was held because she was being loved too much. She cried when she was alone because she needed to know that she was loved. She cried in her pram because she was being shaken and vibrated. She cried in the dark folds of the night. She cried in the long haul of the day. Her eyes were searching for a rainbow and she was reaching out for the stars. And her parents tried everything! Yet still she cried, searching for something intangible, which maybe the world could not satisfy.

As she grew, Dotty became more confident. She loved a dark green, knitted doll called Mary Jane and a teddy with only one arm called Teddy. Her tricycle was a chariot and her racetrack took a full circuit round the sofa. She became boisterous and longed for the day when they would leave their upstairs flat and live in a bungalow where she could make as much noise as she liked. With pan lids for orchestral instruments and a passion for banging doors, Dotty was on her way to stardom.

Mummy went away for a while and Dotty stayed with Grandma and Grandpa who loved her and let her eat biscuits. She was allowed to sleep in an enormous, big, high bed and it was fun till, one morning Daddy answered Grandpa's phone and told Dotty that she had a new sister who would be a playmate for her and wouldn't that be fun? Dotty was very excited because she sensed that something special was in the air and everybody was happy.

When Mummy came back to their new bungalow with a tiny baby, Dotty ran around shouting and laughing and jumping all over the furniture and celebrating that she had a sister who would play with her and she would never be lonely again. But the tiny baby made more noise than Dotty was allowed to make, Mummy kept telling Dotty to calm down and stop making a noise, and Daddy was always out at work. Dotty didn't like living in the bungalow anymore because she wasn't allowed to make as much noise as she liked and Mummy seemed only to love the tiny, noisy baby who didn't play with her even once in all these long weeks. And sad to say, Mary Jane had been thrown out during the removal because she was getting a bit shabby.

Dotty stopped being noisy. She stopped being happy. She discovered another world where she could pretend to be a princess and she didn't need Mummy or the little sister who couldn't play with her. She became invisible and tried not to get too excited or too happy and certainly not too sad. Dotty knew that if she looked after herself and didn't expect too much, then she would be just fine.

Dotty played that game for many, many years. Her Daddy had a swing built in the garden and that was where Dotty dreamed her dreams, did her worrying and sometimes let herself feel sad. She lived her imaginary life there but knew that one day she would meet a handsome prince and be very, very content in a far away place. Then she would live happily ever after.

Till then, Dotty would stay out of trouble, if she only could discover how to, and be patient. And if she could only stay invisible...!

Parents are much to be pitied. They just can't get it right no matter how hard they try! I was nurtured and nourished by parents who had nothing but my best interests at heart. My mother is a perfectionist who wanted me to be as good as she could possibly make me and my father was a wonderful provider who grudged me nothing. They brought me up carefully, encouraging what they liked about me and stamping out what they didn't. I was being moulded with an end product in mind.

As a parent myself, I know that I did my best to give my children everything good. I tried so hard to provide them with a secure home where they knew they were loved unconditionally and no matter what they did in the present or the future nothing would change that quality of love. But, years later, I now understand that my daughters didn't necessarily see things as I meant them to. Sometimes love can seem oppressive. Sometimes a parent's concern seems overwhelmingly suffocating to the child. Being a positive, energetic parent can be misunderstood as 'managing' or 'controlling'! Being a laid-back, all-accepting parent can be equally misunderstood.

From the child's point of view, early life can be tough. Picture a new baby, newly ejected from the security of the womb and experiencing this strange kind of life in something they call the world. Babies are born with their own little personalities! You only need to compare two or three newborns to realise how differently they all react. Some seem to leave the womb with their eyes wide open, energetic and curious and aware of everything. Others are sleepy and docile, putting up with the adoration of the crowds, but a little bored and only wanting to sleep. Still others are fractious and complaining, with a grudge against the system that moved them on to this cold planet.

We all start off different. How can that be?

After that weekend course when I discovered that I really did have a personality, I discovered Psalm 139. In this piece of writing, the Psalmist is making a discovery also, the discovery that the living God created him individually. He had just had a 'wow' moment, a moment of illumination, a moment when he just 'saw' it, understood it and was revelling in the fantastic insight that he, even he, had been hand-crafted by the Master Craftsman himself.

> *'You created every part of me;*
> *you put me together in my mother's womb...*
> *When my bones were being formed,*
> *carefully put together in my mother's womb,*
> *when I was growing there in secret,*
> *you knew that I was there—*
> *you saw me before I was born.'*
> Psalm 139:13-16

I also had a 'wow' moment, a moment of insight! I could picture it all in my mind's eye. I saw a developing embryo tucked away safely in the damp, warm darkness of the womb. And I saw the creator of the world, of space and of the whole of creation come and rest in that place. And he seemed to stroke his chin in a wise way and decreed, 'This is going to be my lovely child, Dorothy. I think I should give her blonde hair, lots of it, she'll enjoy that. And big, blue eyes like her human daddy. I will make her a NINE—that's quite a challenge—but I will give her all the wisdom she will need to be able to handle that. I won't give you too much self-esteem, Dorothy, in case you become arrogant. You will do much better if you rely on me. But I will make you gentle and patient because I have some good work for you to do on earth. Grow well now and remember that I will always be right here beside you.'

Could it be? Formed by the one who masterminded the Big Bang, who set the planets in their orbits, who rides on the wind and whispers through the thunder? Could it be?

The Psalmist, in a moment of enlightenment, found himself on his knees in wonder. I too could only gaze into the tranquillity of the summer sky and ask, 'Could it be?' I almost expected a chariot to descend from heaven with the answer—but nothing happened to scare my hesitant soul. Inwardly, however, I remembered the beauty of a sunset and the haunting loveliness of the sea at dusk. The creator had formed the physical strength and awesomeness of the ocean.

The skilled hand of that same creator had produced another work of art. ME!

How dare I criticise this work of art? How dare I tell the Lord of the universe that he had made a few mistakes here, that I was nothing special and could he please change a few characteristics here and there? How dare I, the work of his hand, the inspired work of art that had been crafted and moulded and sculpted, find fault with the cosmic artist? How dare I think that perhaps I knew better than the one who had created human beings to be unique in their spiritual-bodily nature? How dare I?

There were consequences of that discovery. I had to repent! I had despised myself for years, floating in a haze of melancholy, and longing to be like someone else, anyone else, because everyone else was better than I was or could ever be. I had turned away from the goodness that flowed over me and around me every day, hoping that perhaps I could kid other people, myself and God that I was something that I was never designed to be. How arrogant!

And I had to rejoice! It meant that I was not here in my skin by chance! I had been designed to function and perform in a given way, with gifts to use for the benefit of all mankind and for myself. And I had some challenges thrown in to give me a goal in my spiritual life. I had the makings of a good number NINE but I had a lot of work to do before I was the grown-up adult that God wanted to use in His world.

Understanding ourselves. Priceless!

To ponder:

Think back to your earliest memories. Where did you learn to distrust people, or to deny your feelings, or to hide your anger or to run away from your problems? Who taught you to be self-sufficient or to be suspicious of others or hide away from the world?

We are all taught how to 'be' and how 'not to be'. We learn what is expected of us in the first years of our lives from our significant others; parents, carers, teachers and others close to the family.

And we learn what is NOT okay. Have a good think about the following options.

What did YOU learn NOT to be when you were a child?

Did you learn that it was NOT Ok to make mistakes?

Did you learn that it was NOT Ok to have your own needs and wants?

Did you learn that it was NOT Ok to have your own feelings and identity?

Did you learn that it was NOT Ok to function too well or be too happy?

Did you learn that it was NOT Ok to be too comfortable in the world?

Did you learn that it was NOT Ok to trust yourself or others?

Did you learn that it was NOT Ok to trust anyone or be vulnerable yourself?

Did you learn that it was NOT Ok to assert yourself?

- Which one did you grow up to believe?

- Make a list of things you do that are done because you believe that message.

- That was then. This is now. Is that message always true?

- How would your life be different if you challenge the unconscious childhood message and live differently?

Write about this in your journal.

Chapter 6
Meet the Inner Observer

Depression isn't just about unhappiness. Things happen in our bodies and we become physically unwell—without there seeming to be a cause. Things happen in our minds that seem crazy to us when our rational days return.

If I could change only one thing about these days of depression, I would alter my attitude towards myself. In my mind, I turned against myself. Something had happened to me that I didn't understand and I was no longer a likeable person. There was nothing in me to admire. So I turned on myself. Feeling worthless and helpless I told myself what I thought of me—and none of it was good.

The torrents of self-abuse streamed through me every waking moment and often in my dreams. I put myself down, hating that I had to live with myself, shouting abuse and giving myself a mental kicking every time I did something silly. It stemmed from sadness and disappointment. From the dead hopes rotting inside me. From my fear that this was all I could expect in my life and it would never change. And from the years of neglect I had endured at my own hands.

The Enneagram gave me an escape route. Because a neutral observer had told me that I was a gifted, talented NINE with qualities of compassion and understanding and peacemaking, I wanted to believe it. An expert had told me this. She must be right. The Enneagram was a personality profiling system that had been around for centuries, it had to be worth listening to. Had it not been proved to be right, it would have died out.

And I so much longed to believe that there was something—anything—special in me. It sure didn't feel like it from where I was standing! But if I could hold on to the fact that I was generally kind and empathic and understanding, then maybe, just maybe, I could start to believe in myself again.

The tool we need here is called the Inner Observer. This function is vital in the search for wholeness. It is a part of our own awareness, but it seems detached from our real selves. Imagine you could split yourself into two. You—the real, unfathomable you—is within your head and your body, while another part of you can stand outside of you and watch what is going on. This is the Inner

Observer, watching, noticing, seeing perhaps for the first time how you behave, how you think, how you feel. It is a neutral observer. Hurrah for neutral observers! It has no opinion of its own. It simply witnesses and tells us what is going on inside ourselves.

So I was able at last to treat myself with some respect. NINEs are quite nice people—so says the neutral observer! My Inner Observer began to notice that too. Watching myself, I began to see the compassion I had and my desire to connect with people. I became aware of my listening skills, my ability to make people feel good about themselves. How easy it was for me to take charge of situations and direct operations in a firm but kindly way. All this was far from the concept of self that had been around in the last few years. But seeing the positives in my nature reminded me that I had been a worthwhile person at one time, there were still glimpses of it even in the depression, and if this was the REAL me then I would like to discover the rest of the picture.

Being depressed, I could only believe the positives if there was a healthy dose of negatives thrown in. I was highly suspicious of compliments.

But I was in luck there! Plenty of challenges in my nature. Plenty of room for improvement. And the Enneagram was able to give me real things to work on. It did this very clearly but in an encouraging way. It told me that I probably didn't have a huge problem with gluttony—true—I had lost interest in food and almost everything else as well. Nor did I have a problem with lust or envy—I didn't have the energy for either of them. Pride wasn't too much of an issue either—there was nothing left to be proud of. And stinginess didn't play much part in my life, nor laziness as such. But SLOTH! Ahhh, now that was worth looking at, and maybe anger, and deceit. Help...

Sloth definitely felt like the biggest of the problems. I had always thought that laziness and sloth were the same thing, but apparently not. And so, although I am always doing something and my life had always been a busy one, I have been guilty of great sloth, seemingly. I took this badly, as you can imagine. Me, lazy?! Surely not! But it was with this discovery that my life began to change.

So I began to answer this question. Where in my life do I recognize sloth? There were a million answers, all important to the way I had spent my time and to the way I saw myself. And then I put the Inner Observer to work and began to see how active sloth was in my life. The busiest sloth I have ever seen.

The activity of Sloth. No 1

I lived my life in the shallows of the river of chaos. Not the mighty ocean of chaos. I never allowed myself total and absolute chaos. I could always pull back from the brink and fake it (deceit!), allowing people only to see the perfectly dressed, charming hostess or the neat, tidy and well-run household, or the yummy mummy in the high heels at the school gate. No one, not even me, saw the chaos underneath it all. It wasn't worth being organized. I wasn't worth it. I didn't deserve it. I was bad, remember. I couldn't do anything. In fact I was such a miserable specimen that I actually deserved unhappiness. So I created it for myself, without even knowing I was doing it. Now that's clever! That's sloth.

Failure to attend to myself was the sloth that the Enneagram was pointing out here. And it was so true. Why had I never seen it before? Tracing it back to its roots I had to go back to a childhood where I didn't get any brownie points.

Not for good marks at school, 'What did Ian Sharp get for his spelling test? Were you as good as him?'

Not for being helpful around the house, 'I don't know why I allowed you to do the dusting. You never do it right.'

Not for being a good, polite child because I was a surly, secretive one who never smiled or chatted or got to know my parents.

So I gave up on myself at an early age. I simply wasn't worth the bother! That was perhaps understandable but nevertheless it was unhelpful and slothful and my Inner Observer clocked it up. Why, forty years later, had I become depressed? Hmmm. I wonder if it had anything to do with my failure to attend to myself?

The activity of sloth. No 2

I know people who are inner directed know exactly where they want to go and what they want to do. My husband is like that. So are most of his colleagues. I used to child-mind for similar people who knew their worth and their purpose and got on with it without much of a backward glance. I had made such an art form out of my sloth that I scoffed slightly at these driven workaholics who didn't have time to smell the roses or enjoy a sunset. Slow down, I used to tell them. Enjoy the journey. Don't rush headlong to the finishing line. There's a world to be enjoyed out here, outside of the workplace.

I wonder if secretly I believed that these people were a bit selfish—work, work, working all the hours they could. Look at me, I wanted to say. I live for other people. I never do anything for myself. I pour every drop of energy into my home. My husband and children come first. Then I see to my friends and neighbours. I attend to others. That's my mission statement. You should try it sometime.

The Inner Observer was quick to flag up a few things here. I realized, with its help, that it was much easier for me to attend to other people's agendas because it removed the need to pursue my own agenda. What agenda would that be, I wonder. I didn't have a personal agenda and I didn't want one. I was happy attending to everyone else. It was easy this way. A day could be lived without thinking of me except in a dreamy, unreal way that was like a hazy, shimmering suggestion somewhere just outside of my awareness.

A typical day would see me bundling my own and my sister's children into a car that was far too small, along with two dogs. Off to school through the chaos of Edinburgh's rush hour. Then a walk on Cramond foreshore with the dogs. This would have been my favourite part of the day, if only I hadn't had to attend to the dogs. Then a quick clear up in the house before I would set off on the morning project, which would inevitably involve a friend or a neighbour. The other person would likely have suggested these jaunts; so slothful would I be that I would have no ideas about what I wanted or needed to do.

Then school pick-ups, a house full of children belonging to working mums and neighbours—and my own. Then dinner; homework; dog-walking; bedtime; into the bath; soak; doze; and bed.

I prided myself on having no needs of my own. My idealized self-image was that I was there in the world to see to whoever needed me, so long as no effort was required of me. I would spend time with you, I would listen to you, empathise, sympathise, pass on to you all my slothful wisdom and then drift on to the next person who would also be willing to waste time with me.

My own agenda was lost. If you neglect someone for long enough they will just fade away. I had neglected myself. Eventually, I faded away too.

The activity of sloth. No 3

Agreeing with people. 'You do it all the time,' noticed the Inner Observer. Well, of course I do. It's polite. And if I disagreed they might argue with me. So what if they argued with me, you might ask? Well, I don't like arguments. So I would avoid getting into one. Except if I thought it might be fun, that is. I quite like a bit of banter and confrontational intimacy. But I can't handle hostility, not even a teensy-weensy bit!

The Inner Observer had noticed something vital here. So terrified was I of opening up a disagreement that I would agree with almost everything—in public, at any rate—or stay very quiet while the conversation was going on. I would even agree to do things while my insides were screaming at me, 'Don't do it. You will regret that! You know how much you hate doing that kind of thing.' But I couldn't risk an argument with someone because they might end up disliking me. Or I would come over as being selfish. I couldn't risk doing that.

Well spotted, Inner Observer. That had to change. I began to ask myself, 'Do you agree with that point of view? Is there anything else you would like to say here?' So screwing up all my courage, I began to take a position on things. The first time I did this, I expected the world to stop, everyone to gasp and frown and viciously turn on me. I was even holding my breath waiting for the avalanche of disapproval. I couldn't believe the response I got. My point of view was acknowledged—with thanks from the chairperson, I may add—and the discussion moved on. The world had not stopped. The sky had not fallen down. I hadn't been struck down by a bolt of lightning. But I had been 'selfish' enough to state my case. And it felt good. I had taken back a little bit of control over my situation. And I would try this again.

I began to realize how rarely I faced anything if it involved any form of conflict. Therefore nothing was ever dealt with in my world. And I had to live with the consequences of my sloth. I became very 'stuck', powerless, helpless, trapped, and depressed.

The activity of sloth. No 4

'You say "yes" to everything,' So said the inner Observer one day.

'Rubbish,' I replied. 'I rebel against everything! I'm always saying no. No, I don't want to do that. No, I certainly will not be going there. No, I am not even going to consider getting involved in that.'

'But you SAY 'yes' to everything,' repeated the Inner Observer.

Oh yes, so I do. I rebel inwardly, of course. I very often KNOW what I don't want. But since I rarely know what it is that I DO want, I have no answer but to say 'yes'. So I get involved in whatever it is and three days or weeks or months down the line I am screaming for release. Let me out of here. I hate this. I never wanted to do it anyway. But since NINEs only feel good if their loved ones feel good, it is so hard to turn down requests from them.

So I had said 'yes'. Better to have said 'no', risked the possible conflict at the time, and moved on. But usually by the time I realize that I really can't do this, it is too late and I am in so deep that the resulting conflict is much harder to deal with. I therefore make myself thoroughly unpopular. Of course I can't handle the disapproval and criticism rightly leveled at me and I feel so bad! I hate myself for it. My inner comfort disintegrates. So I disappear into myself for a few days or weeks to lick my wounds and recover—failure again.

You are right, Inner Observer. I DO say 'yes' to everything. I am too slothful to say 'no' and deal with the consequences in a grown-up way. I still react like the child I was. I have always coped with my aggression by ignoring it. I'm good at that. That has to change.

Real development means risking the discomfort of conflict, even aggression. We have to be prepared to jeopardise our inner comfort for a time while we take a good, hard look at reality. We will get used to this way of thinking and working. We will even be grateful we have learned to say 'no'. Because it makes us feel awake and alive again. It gives us choices. That is a novelty we will come to love.

The activity of sloth—Oh no, maybe this is not SLOTH after all!

When I was four, the time came for me to go to school. In those days before nursery schools, we little ones had no concept of what school was. Everyone said I would love it there. So I imagined what school would be like if it was something I was going to love. What would I love?. I decided, after many long hours of daydreaming, that I would really love to sit on red velvet sofas all day, drink tea (which I had never tasted, but it certainly sounded like the kind of thing you do in a happy world), and chat to people, all day, every day. That is what I would like most in the whole world.

As you can imagine, the reality of school came as a huge shock and disappointment!

It is interesting that a whole lifetime later this is how I make my living. In the work of Life Coaching and Spiritual Direction I spend hours and hours with people, drinking tea and chatting. In one particular hotel in Edinburgh where I often meet clients, they have even provided me with red velvet sofas—a dream come true!

The Inner Observer has helped me to see that the flip side of this coin named Sloth is happy attentiveness. It is my relaxed, contented spirit that delights in spending dedicated time journeying with people. This is my gift and part of the package the Master of the universe created in me at the moment of my conception.

I remember gardening in our huge, overgrown garden in Perthshire. In one unrecognisable flowerbed I found the struggling remains of a yellow flower losing its battle against the weed-infested, dried out scrubland. Everything else in the vicinity had long since succumbed to death by strangulation. This survivor was known as yellow loosestrife, a plant that gardeners despise because it is common and can be grown anywhere, no matter how poor the soil is. I guess that's the only reason it was still surviving. Not a sophisticated plant!

But, in my ignorance, I loved it. It was a ray of bright sunshine in a poverty-stricken patch of ground. So I carefully dug it up, spent twenty minutes disentangling the roots of the plant from the roots of a dozen other weedy thugs and then took the poor wee thing to the tap and ran water over the long white roots till they were clean and I was sure that no trace of the strangling weed roots were left entangled in it.

Only then could I replant it in a newly prepared patch of ground, created especially for it. No more struggle for my prized, rescued, beautiful plant! And it thrived. I had given it clean soil with lots of nutrients and ensured it had plenty of light and water—all it needed for growth. It grew high and thick and beautiful and lit up its surroundings. It was later split up and replanted all over the garden and even moved house with us some years later.

The Enneagram was and still is such a useful tool in tackling my weed-infested soul. I needed all this sloth pointing out to me. I needed to clean up my act, and to look again at my roots. So much rubbish needed to be removed and discarded. It helped me to see the beautiful person I could grow into, a person I never believed could be me.

I had an image in my mind's eye of God, the master gardener, lifting me up and putting me in a sieve, pouring gallons of water over me and gently massaging my roots till I was clean.

And then He said, 'Now, Dorothy, I can use you!'

Another tool. Watching yourself and making the changes.

To ponder:

The Enneagram system of personality describes nine different ways of 'being' or nine personalities. Have a look at these brief descriptors and see which one seems to describe you best.

Type ONE: The Perfectionist. Ernest, ethical, idealistic, orderly, self-disciplined, high moral standards. Can be judgemental, inflexible, critical and controlling.

Type TWO: The Helper. Out-going, caring, loving, generous, tuned in to how others feel. Can be martyr-like, possessive, manipulative and overly demonstrative.

Type THREE: The Achiever. Confident, efficient, self-propelled, industrious, energetic. Can be overly competitive, vain, workaholic and selfish with their time.

Type FOUR: The Artist/Romantic. Creative, sensitive, emotional, stylish in a 'one-off' way. Can be dreamy, self-conscious, moody, self-absorbed and very dramatic.

Type FIVE: The Observer. Introvert, analytical, objective, curious, knowledgeable, perceptive. Can be distant, stubborn, stingy and intellectually arrogant.

Type SIX: The Stabilizer. Loyal, sensible, practical, responsible, committed, meticulous. Can be fearful, hyper-vigilant, defensive and rigid.

Type SEVEN: The Adventurer. Energetic, fun-loving, enthusiastic, spontaneous, confident. Can be self-centred, rebellious, impulsive, restless and greedy for life.

Type EIGHT: The Asserter. Confident, assertive, direct, energetic, argumentative yet protective of the underdog. Can be bossy, controlling, domineering and aggressive.

Type NINE: The Peacemaker. Open-minded, peaceful, receptive, gentle and understanding. Can be spaced-out, vague, apathetic, stubborn and passive-aggressive.

Chapter 7
Trauma

A life devoid of trauma is an impoverished life. It is true that none of us seek trouble nor willingly co-operate with it when it hits our lives but without the opportunity to engage in the struggle for survival our lives would end up poorer. It seems that we don't 'make hay while the sun shines'. Nor do we 'mend our sails in fine weather'. We take the good times for granted, coast through most of our lives and learn nothing unless we absolutely are forced into it.

I was very impressed with the manager of a top English rugby club who had been slogging through the marshlands of defeat and failure for more than two years, encouraging a young team to take the knocks and work hard to make use of the struggle. When interviewed, he shrugged and shook his head but answered his critics by saying, 'Good times don't build character!' And so, by inference, he was telling us that the bad times they were currently experiencing were going to be important in determining the kind of future they were to have. Their recovery and subsequent success would be at least partly brought about by the way they were engaging with that prolonged time of failure.

This is not a lesson any of us want to know about. We just don't want to hear! We don't want bad times. We have no desire to learn valuable lessons if it means we have to lose a beloved family member to cancer or be made redundant or become ill ourselves. We don't care that we will come out the other end stronger. We would rather stay weak, quite frankly! Ok, these experiences might be enriching, force open our vision, enlarge our minds, and deepen our understanding. But we would rather cocoon ourselves in safety and comfort, risking nothing, gaining nothing, but also, losing nothing.

And yet, although we try to look right through trouble and ignore it for as long as possible, we all find that it catches up eventually. It is the fundamental human condition. We all have our troubles, one way or another. No one lives a charmed life. We all have to face up to trouble and, if we are clever, learn to use it to our advantage.

My life at this point had run into the ground. I hadn't done anything wrong in the world's eyes. I hadn't cheated on my husband nor beaten the kids. I hadn't embezzled money nor murdered my brother. I didn't gossip or lie or steal from the local supermarket. I was trying to be good, to do the best I could and live an exemplary life in so far as I was able. So why was I ill? It wasn't fair.

6th October

I think I have made a discovery!

Until this weekend I thought that God had left me. But now I'm wondering. What if all that is happening to me is known to God? What if I am going through all this—depression, or whatever it is—and he knows all about it?

That would mean one of two things. Either he knows and doesn't really care what's going on, or—and this is the interesting bit!—He knows what's going on and he DOES care, he might be watching from afar, and maybe keeping an eye on the situation in case I need help. What if?!

The sermon was about the 23rd Psalm and as I was listening I was trying to picture it in my imagination. I could see a rocky valley—'the valley of the shadow of death'—and this feels like death so it is quite appropriate really. I was there in the picture but the shepherd and all the sheep seemed to have gone through a split in the rocks at the end of the valley and I was alone. Then the preacher said that even if we felt alone the shepherd would be watching from a distance, trusting us to find our own way but watching out in case we needed his help. So I could picture a shepherd high up on the rocks watching out for me.

I know this is just in my imagination but it did help me to move on in my thinking. Until now I have just felt completely alone, unloved, un-cared for, discarded and fit for nothing in life. But now I wonder. Could it be that God knows, cares, and is watching out for me?

But this then begs the question WHY? Why, if he is a loving God, is he sitting back in heaven letting me suffer this horrendous loss of confidence and not doing anything about it? WHY? I am dying here! Maybe not physically dying but I certainly feel that this is akin to dying. Just disappearing, fading away, and not existing any more. So why doesn't He DO SOMETHING?

9th *October*

The countryside is beautiful. The trees are just beginning to turn into their autumn colours, all the greenery by the riverside is dying down and the town is much quieter with the visitors away home.

But I am still stuck in that valley of death and asking why! You know, I have a feeling that there might be a purpose in all this. Nothing is for nothing. And God doesn't just walk off and forget. The prophet Isaiah asks, 'Can a mother forget her child?' Then he goes on to say that even if she did, the Lord would take care of us. Could that be true? Could this valley be known to God and could he be using the experience to grow me into a stronger person?

I wish I could believe it!

14th October

Julian of Norwich. I had never heard of this lady—in fact I thought with a name like Julian she was a man. She is quite famous apparently. She was a 14th century anchorite who was sealed into a room in a church in Norwich and spent her days writing, thinking, praying and listening to people in need. Quite a lady. Here is one of the things she says. Very encouraging!

Julian of Norwich says that it is 'needful' to every man (and woman too presumably)...sometimes to be in comfort and sometimes to fail and be left to him or herself. God wills that he keeps us safe anyway— 'ever alike', in her words—'in weal and in woe and loves us as much in woe as in weal.' And sometimes for the 'profit of our souls' we are left to ourselves even if sin is not the cause. She then talks about how she felt she had been left alone and it had nothing to do with sin. But, she says, God freely gives weal when it pleases him and suffers us to be in woe sometimes, and both is because he loves us so much. For it is God's will that we are held by him in comfort. Bliss is lasting, without end, whereas pain is passing and shall be brought to naught.

A lot to think about here. What if it is true that God holds us in woe every bit as tightly as when we are in weal? So is he holding me now—definitely in woe! Maybe he is. And if he is aware of my woe and is holding me through it, he may again bring me to a time of 'weal'.

So,'weal and woe' are alike to God
He is 'keeping' us whether we are in weal or in woe
Pain is passing—Julian is inferring that it's not even very important.
The 'woe' might even be for the 'profit of my soul'.

I would love to know that this time of 'woe' would count for something, that it wasn't just a waste of all these months and years of my life.

'Pain is passing' she says, like childbirth. Once the new life is born you forget the pain. In fact you feel that the pain has been more than worth it for the happy outcome! Could it be possible that the new life will be the new, improved version of me? The me that God wants me to be. The person he had in mind when I was born. The super special, deluxe version that maybe I could become one day? It would almost be worth it then; worth the emptiness, the sadness, the loss of confidence. I wonder!

Nothing is wasted in God. He is the master re-user. Recycling our experience is his game. He takes the rubbish we create in our lives, mixes it with a few other experiences, tosses it all around for a while and carefully crafts a brand new shape, texture and design. Eureka! All things are made new! It would have to be admitted that it is a very painful experience but if, at the end of it all, our lives are dross-free, connected and more satisfying, then it might just be worth it. This was a major shift in how I understood what was going on and I was grateful to the wisdom of Mother Julian echoing down the centuries to meet my need on that day.

Isn't it strange that our search seems always to be towards happiness and freedom, connectedness, peace, significance and acceptance. Yet life's experience almost never proves this to be possible. What we get seems to be one big character-building experience! We must learn to appreciate that the bad times are as useful as the good times. Then we could learn to embrace them as the architects of our future.

We are most likely to gripe and fight against the time of woe instead of embracing it as a positive experience. Many thousands of us do. I certainly did in these bad old days of depression. I found it almost impossible to accept that my experience of woe could be as positive and as useful as the times of weal.

I started people-watching. I watched carefully and saw that when they (or maybe I should say 'we') resist our woe and fight against our seemingly negative circumstances, we sink into gloom and develop a vocabulary consisting of 'moaning' words. We adopt a certain tense set to our facial muscles. Our entire mindset expects trouble. We shake our heads a lot, sympathising with ourselves and bemoaning the fact that our negative attitude had been right again. We grow into copies of Eeyore in the A.A. Milne stories. We expect the worst and we generally get it! We contract into ourselves and tense ourselves against the enemy—which is life itself!

Julian of Norwich seemed to be suggesting that we have a choice here.

We can tense ourselves against the onslaught or we can learn to welcome adversity and positively look for all the side-benefits it brings. In the end, it may help the whole process if we put our energies into 'going with the flow' and learning the system of life so that we can get the most out of it.

When my children were young they were highly amused by my attitude to windy days by the sea. When they complained about the strength of the cold wind I would tell them just to relax and let the wind blow right through them. That way they would feel they were a part of the weather and enjoy its mood instead of fighting against it and finding inevitably that it would win and beat them down.

Walking through life is just the same. But to tackle life in that way we need tools for the journey. 'Give me a fulcrum,' Archimedes is reported to have said, 'and a place to stand—and I will move the world.' Any of the tools in this book can be our fulcrum. The decision to take a stand has to be your own. The place to stand is right here. There is no better time.

Then we can begin to tackle life so that we are no longer blown away by it or left breathless from fighting against it. These tools will help us to relax into life, fear the future less and be able to welcome what is just around the corner. Whatever it is, the future belongs to God and with him we need fear nothing.

So here is another tool—trusting that God is in it all, good or bad.

To ponder:

> Lord, I have given up my pride and turned away from my arrogance. I am not concerned with great matters or with subjects too difficult for me. Instead, I am content and at peace. As a child lies quietly in its mother's arms, so my heart is quiet within me. Israel, trust in the Lord now and forever!
> (Psalm 131:1-3)

Chapter 8
Images

Who is God? What is he—or she? How do I know anything about him?[2]

Who am I? What makes up this human being I recognise as 'me'? What makes me different from you? How did I become who or what I am?

We are born knowing nothing of either God or ourselves. We built our own pictures. It all came out of our own heads. We made ourselves up. We made God up. We are a creation of our own fantasies! Yes? No?

I guess all psychologists would agree that we are born with certain pre-suppositions within the essence of the real self. These are the building blocks that help us grow into the best that we can be.

They may also agree that what happens to us in the first years of our lives shape the way we grow up and see ourselves as individuals. We react to life events, to the way we are treated by the adults around

---

[2] Let's call him a man, shall we? It doesn't really matter because surely God is above gender but we have to call him something, so 'male' he is for the sake of simplicity

us, we learn to defend ourselves in certain ways that seem to help us and we develop ways of being that seem to us the most useful ways to behave.

Other than that, it's pretty much up to us. We listen to what we are told about ourselves, we imagine what we must be like if these things are true—and, hey, presto, we have an identity! Children can shape-shift and recreate themselves all the time until they settle in to a way of being themselves. That then becomes pretty well fixed.

I was told as a child that I was difficult. I remember being compared to my younger, sweeter sister and I certainly came off worse. I think that comment, perhaps only said once, became part of my identity. I was four at the time. And I had to use my imagination to understand what the word 'difficult' said about me. I made it up in my imagination. Then, I think, I lived up to the description. A difficult girl goes her own way, does her own thing without noticing what the adults are saying to her, she should be headstrong and opinionated and completely unreliable.

In living up to the 'difficult' label, I lost sight of what I really wanted to be and what needed to be done to form my character. I became lost. I certainly succeeded in building the ego but in doing so I lost sight of the real me, the one buried deep inside and wanting to blossom and grow. I had to wait till I was forty before I could strip it all down and rediscover me, the one that got lost under the 'difficult' label.

I was told that I was just like my father's side of the family. I had their sharp tongue! I suspect this was not a compliment. But I rather liked my father's side of the family. It seemed to me that they had more fun than we had. They were witty and more worldly wise and lived in the city. So I copied them and felt sophisticated. Not my mother's desired outcome!

My sister, on the other hand, was being 'sweet', she lived up to that expectation and continued to be sweet with all the foreseeable consequences. A sweet girl would never become angry, would never force her opinions on to people, always fitted in and disregarded her own agenda and remained pleasant in all circumstances. She also, in adulthood, needed to rediscover the unacknowledged part of herself. That had little to do with 'sweet' and all to do with focus, determination and dogged pursuit of her previously disregarded inner agenda.

And we both have had a few 'anger' issues to resolve. Anger was never allowed in our family. Neither were loud voices, bad language, nor our playground dialect. I had real problems living up to all that and being 'difficult' at the same time. So I had to redouble my efforts to live up to expectations. And never having been allowed to express anger, meant we had to work hard on finding what anger meant and appropriate ways of using and expressing it years later.

The way we are treated by our significant adults is vital. If we are cherished, protected and treated tenderly we will grow up very differently than if we are neglected, bullied and exposed to the world's rougher side. Our 'essence' is not changed. We are what we are, deep inside. But as we react and adjust to the way we are treated, we grow up differently.

We each find ways of defending ourselves from the realities of our own worlds. For me, the defence mechanism I used most was 'narcotisation'. That means that I found ways of being absent from myself and from my real world in order to remain content. I became 'spaced out'.

For you it will be different. There are many ways of protecting ourselves.

I was nine years old and it had been a beautiful summer's day. I didn't understand what I had done. But it was very bad, whatever it was. My Mum had been really, really angry and I was sure she hated me. I was left in my bedroom where I huddled down on a little Indian mat my dad had sent home when he was in the Air Force in India. I was so sad and upset because she didn't like me, I was a disappointment to her, I never got anything right and I was hopeless. After the tears had dried up and I realised that she had forgotten about me and I would miss a whole afternoon with my friends, I began to daydream.

Dreams kept me going. Some day I would be loved. Someone would really want to look after me and cherish me. That person would adore me and tell me how special I was. I would be happy and I might even have children in these dreams and I would never lock them in a cold bedroom without them knowing why. I would love them the way I wanted to be loved myself.

I could dream for hours at a time. Sometimes I couldn't get to sleep at night because these dreams were so comfortable. If I slept, I would wake up too soon to the realities of my life. But if I stayed in my dream world then I would be happy. So much of my childhood was spent in another world, one of comfort, peace, happiness, outside my own physical world. That was 'narcotisation', my chosen defence mechanism.

We don't want to experience pain in any way, but we all must. Usually it is emotional pain, but sometimes it is physical. Since we don't want to deal with the pain we use a strategy—a defence, a protective barrier that will come between the feeling and our conscious awareness of it. It will keep us safe from the feeling. It distorts reality for a short time in order to help us keep our balance.

Our image of God is built up in a similar way. We use our imaginations. We listen to what adults tell us. Often they have no idea themselves, so our information is at best partial and at worst totally wrong. We often listen for the characteristics God is supposed to have, we look around for a possible role model, and then we make up our picture—a photo-fit, lookalike jigsaw. Which is probably more wrong than right but better than nothing, or so we think.

Jesus was like God, they told me. I liked Jesus, he was a really nice person, he told stories and I loved stories. He had friends and seemed to wander around the country with them. He never worried about anything. His weather was always sunny. Everything seemed complete in his world.

But God seemed to be different from Jesus. We sang a hymn in school that said,

'God is always near me, hearing what I say...' This was scary. I was difficult, remember, and if he was like other adults then he wouldn't like 'difficult'. So he wouldn't like me. And by that time I had become so complete in my 'difficultness' that I couldn't be anything else.

We are children when we learn most about our faith. We breathe in our parents' beliefs, which may or may not have worked for them. We 'get the idea' from grown-ups who may or may not have it right. We listen to Bible stories and usually the reader of these stories has a point to make at the end. And we hear the moral, but miss out on contact with the writer.

In looking around for look-alike types I put together a picture of God. He actually wasn't like Jesus at all. People must have got that wrong.

In my head he was much more like the dragon of a teacher who taught me for two years when I was eight or nine. The belt or the 'tawse'[3] was her chosen instrument of torture, and she ensured that we learned by rote a passage of scripture every week—or else we were beaten.

Or God was like my grandfather who ran a haulage business from his wheelchair, scaring every employee within an inch of their lives.

Or God might be like my dad, a lovely, patient man but so disappointed in us when we let him down.

And he was probably like Mr Barclay, our headmaster, who was stiff and formal, and seemed to speak in riddles—and a posh accent!

I didn't feel at all happy about this God I was inventing. I was scared of him quite frankly. So I

---

[3] The tawse is an implement used for corporal punishment. It was used for educational discipline in Scotland.

decided to keep my distance from him. I went to Church as that's what families did in those days. But I didn't take God too seriously because he probably wouldn't like me.

And so this continued well into adulthood. God was a big scary man who expected too much. I thought he had very strict rules and I never managed to obey them all. But I tried. And I expected other people to try too. And if we all did our best maybe someday God would change his mind about us and like us.

Who would want anything to do with a God like that? Nobody! With a God like that how would religion ever have got off the ground? Never! So, maybe I was wrong.

In later years I discovered that deeply buried inside me is a contemplative, waiting to get out and live. I love the mystery of God, the fact that even our best guesses are likely to be completely and totally wrong. I believe and feel sure that God is fantastically wonderful, huge, powerful, the uncreated, riding on the wings of the wind and author of the universe. And yet, without our awareness, he dwells in the deepest part of us, bringing us to life, alive in the very air we breathe. He is huge, magnificent and awesome but closer to each of us than our thoughts. Loving us, whom he created out of nothing, hovering over us and tenderly waiting for us to find him within. That is a God worthy of our attention.

But you know, it is so hard to get a glimpse of this all-powerful but utterly wonderful God. When I was a young mum I tried so hard to build up a new adult picture of him because I wanted to teach my children. But it seemed that whatever he was like, he certainly wasn't playing ball with me. My prayers were either 'please' or rants, depending on the mood of the day. But I did pray. I really did believe. My faith kept me going rather than any certainties. My knowledge of the bible helped. Speaking to older, wiser God-people also encouraged me to keep on searching. But there seemed little evidence that would have convinced anyone.

On holiday one summer, struggling to enjoy some relaxation and coping with three children under six, I came to the end of my energy. I was so tired I wanted to crawl away on my own and just cry. I felt I had no energy left. I couldn't do this any more. I was a hopeless mother, a terrible wife and, in fact, a pretty bad all-rounder. The world had its expectations. My family had its expectations. I thought that even my husband had his expectations. I couldn't do all the things I was expected to do and so my prayer was one of desperation.

'All I want,' I whimpered, 'is to be a good wife and mother.'

For the first time ever, I heard a whisper in my head that said, 'And that's all I ask of you.'

It was a God voice. I had never heard it before, but when it came I recognised it in an instant. The voice of the God who flung stars into space, who lights up the aurora borealis and thunders through the earthquake—this God was speaking to me. He knew I was there. He had heard my whimper. He made himself known to me. He wasn't scary. He wasn't making demands. He was just there where I needed him, telling me what I needed to hear, cutting through all the crap of the world's expectations. In a sentence, he brought me to rest. I could do that. I could be a good wife and mother. If that was all I had to do, I was sorted. Whew! Thank you God.

It was like switching a light on in a dark room. I began to see things in the dark. And the more I saw, the more I was able to walk through the room without falling and with growing confidence.

More recently I have become aware of the resurgence of Celtic spirituality, an ancient way of living with a natural spiritual dimension to daily life. This I love. The Celts lived on the fringes of this country around the 4th and 5th centuries and practised Druid nature mysticism. They believed that it was possible, natural even, to be in communion with something far greater than themselves. They saw through the eyes of the soul that their gods moved around on the same soil as they did and spoke in the wind. They respected every part of the natural world, revering it and recognising in it the very breath of divine presence. They were an intuitive people and used their insights as much as they used rational thought. A sixth sense was more important than the usual five we seem to rely on today.

I first came across Celtic spirituality during a winter in Perthshire—cold, very cold! The snow was thick and the temperature barely registering on any thermometer. We lived on a hill; in fact the whole town of Crieff is built on a hill, and walking to work at the conference centre each day was a full-scale polar expedition—like the Arctic, but without the huskies. Our New Year conference was a full house and our ninety guests were glorying in the beauty of the highland scenery, relishing every moment, outside and in. They were just loving the snowy grandeur. I was free of duties one afternoon and while a huge percentage of mad people wanted to climb the Knock, our local mountain, I opted for a workshop on Celtic spirituality. I really wasn't that interested in the subject matter but anything seemed preferable to a hike in the snow to the top of the world.

And that day I heard much more than a history lecture. I learned of a people, far distant in time, who inhabited the outer fringes of the British Isles. Their gods were many and plentiful and lived in the woods and the rivers, in the rays of the sun and the rhythm of the tides. This was a people who lived close to nature, respected it greatly as the means of their daily sustenance and took great care not to disturb the gods whose dwelling was in each created thing.

Where the Celts first heard of the Christian God, the Lord Jesus and the work of the Holy Spirit is pretty much shrouded in the mists of time. But it would probably be through the Roman occupation of many parts of Britain that the first stories came to be known. And without fuss or fight the Gospel was preached and accepted. Christianity had slowly crept westward to reach the most remote of Scottish communities.

The history of the Celtic people is only sparsely recorded. But the evidence of the centuries seems to suggest that the early missionaries, who introduced Christianity to them, did so very gently. There seemed to be little of the aggression associated with a 'holy' war.

The many beautiful Celtic standing stones tell their own story. Unwilling to stand against these communities the Christians took the solar wheel of the Druid religion and simply superimposed the cross of Christ on its significant shape. The Celtic cross was born. It declares a meeting of two minds, rather than one religion dominating another.

I liked that. Being peace-loving myself I have always been embarrassed by the stories of the Crusades and early missionary endeavours in Africa. Why did Christians think it necessary to fight? Didn't Jesus say that he came to earth to bring peace, not the sword? Wasn't his birth announced by a host of angels proclaiming that he had come to bring peace to earth?

And so, as an adult, I have built up a very different picture of God. The childhood one was totally inaccurate and in no way big enough for my adult needs. It had to be re-assessed. And now it is growing and changing all the time. This God is not simple to understand and it is only in living with him that I am growing in understanding and respect for him. Since that day when he whispered his reassurance to a tired, frustrated, young mum I have never doubted his love, his desire to be part of my life nor my responsibility to him to be the best that I can be. If he is the one who created me then I want to be the person he dreamt of at the moment of my conception. I don't need to be a star, a success or a giant in my world. But I do need to be me—for God's sake.

To ponder:

Whatever your lifestyle, I encourage you to find a little regular patch of silence and aloneness.

• Find a quiet, easily accessible place for your 'quiet time'. For me it is a chair that faces out to the garden. Or sometimes a particular rocky spot on the beach near my house.

• Settle yourself using whatever help you need—music, a ticking clock, a singing bowl.

• Settle into that place inside of yourself where you go to be alone. Invite God to join you.

• Spend a few minutes just sitting together, being together, with no need to talk, although you may do so if you want. Just breathe deeply and relax. Enjoy the safe and sacred space you have created within yourself.

In making this a habit, you are opening yourself to new realisations—of yourself and also of the God who walks unseen beside you. Make friends. Be still together often.

Chapter 9
Scripture to go

With a God like this in my life, I would never be quite the same again. The changes were insignificant at first; slow changes inside myself rather than anything to be noticed by the world at large. I was calmer. This God had taken an interest in me, had spoken into my situation, completely out of the blue. I was so excited by that! I still knew pretty well nothing about him. But I was now sure of two things: he DID exist, otherwise who had been speaking to me in such a loving and reassuring way and he WAS interested in me even though I felt I was far too boring for anyone with any sense to care.

I began to speak to him. I spoke to the voice that I had heard, not to the picture of God I had built up as a child. That God hadn't been real after all, he was just a figment of my imagination. I read about him in the bible and realised that an awful lot of people had made the same mistake as I had. The Old Testament in particular is full of stories of God trying to get to know people but they went rushing off in fear and did stupid things. They didn't get to know what he is really like. They had made him up in their imaginations, thought he was scary and tried to live without him.

The same thing happened in Jesus' stories in the New Testament. He tried to tell them what God was REALLY like but nobody listened, except for a few who stuck by Jesus and learned a lot from him.

During the depression years, my new picture of the God who cares was to be severely tested. This is often the time when you hear people say, 'So where's your God now?'

Well he was still there, not in any recognisable form but somewhere in the background, watching while I ran headlong at a brick wall and shattered into pieces. I couldn't see him at the time. I probably wasn't even giving him any thought, so busy was I trying to scrape together the remnants of my pride and appear normal. As normal as a headless chicken on tranquillisers, that is.

But in spite of the depression taking over my mind and body, I knew that God was aware of the situation because of something that had happened just before we moved house to that frozen land of quiet despair. It was a shaft of light from heaven, a beacon of hope, a twinkle in a summer's evening that assured me that God knew my misery about moving house again and was already in the situation. He didn't bother to tell me that I would end up a messy lump of emotion in a few months time. But he did tell me a story to help me cope. Here is what happened.

I had gone to bed early one evening with a pile of books. In fact, Peter was out and my three girls were still finishing homework or getting ready for bed. I opened my bible, just at random, because I really didn't know what I should be looking for. And I found the story of Jeremiah, which I'm absolutely sure I had never read before. I think I knew vaguely that Jeremiah was a prophet to the Jews thousands of years ago but that was all. Not a popular man, by all accounts, but one who spoke the truth as he saw it and believed he was speaking God's word into the society of his day. I began to read part of it and it turned out to be a letter that Jeremiah wrote to a lot of Jews who had been taken prisoner and herded off to Babylon, wherever that was. And the letter was amazingly appropriate for my situation! It was an instruction manual—'how to live happily in a place you never wanted to go to'.

When I had read it through I found myself chuckling. It was as if God was saying, 'Yes, I know you don't want to move your life and start all over again. The Jews didn't much want to go to Babylon either.

But you can make a success of it just like they did. Here are a few guidelines.' And the chapter went on to list all the things the Jews should do—things like planting gardens, growing their own vegetables, having babies, marrying off their sons and daughters, working for the good of the community etc. It really was amazingly accurate for our situation and seemed quite funny!

But the really good bit was still to come. Towards the end of all these instructions I read.

'When Babylonia's seventy years are over, I will show my concern for you and keep my promise to bring you back home.' Hurrah! We can come back home—albeit seventy years from now!

But that was great. Having read all that, and by then feeling secure with this new, improved version of God, I felt I could live with the immense changes about to happen in our lives. I think that night was a little miracle. It was God intervening, just a wee bit, but enough to assure me that he was 'on the case'. He was asking us to do something not very much to our taste—nor was Babylonia to the Jews' taste—but he was reassuring us that he would be with us in that place of 'exile', in Perthshire in our case.

This had been a turning point. After that night, when I discovered Jeremiah, I turned my face towards the challenge and began to plan for the years ahead, years in exile, far from all the securities I had come to rely on.

I had discovered one of the ancient tools I would be in need of for the rest of my life—God's written word, encouragement to go!

Several years after our time in exile in the Perthshire version of Babylon, I learned another way to discern the way ahead. We had been back in the city for ten years. The drugs my body needed, drugs essential to my eventual recovery, had alleviated the depression by that time. In these ten years I had worked hard to understand what depression was all about; why it happened to me, how I could survive it if it was to continue returning, what changes I needed to make in order to live a healthy life.

I was not cured. Are depressives ever cured? Like alcoholics, workaholics, asthma sufferers and diabetics our condition can only ever be 'under control'. And we work hard to keep it that way. But it needs managing. It needs keeping an eye on. But I was doing all the right things. And I was well.

Knowing by then that our world either shrinks or expands according to our courage, I was determined to move on, out of the depression, into the next phase of life that was surely not going to be dominated by my mental health. I wanted to experience fun, success, life in all its fullness. A poor self-image had robbed me of success in my young years. Depression had robbed me of happiness in my middle years. It was time to step into the future with courage. Time to become the person God intended when he planned my birth from before the dawn of time.

And so we moved house. Again! But this time we wanted to go. A hop, skip and a jump across the Forth estuary to Anstruther, a lovely wee fishing village in the East Neuk of Fife, as far east as you can go and just a few miles before the road drops into the sea at Fife Ness. This was another exile, but this time it was of our own choosing.

No matter how much you love a new house, a new town, new adventures, all that new-ness causes disconnection and disorientation. I began to feel that all my certainties were slipping away from me again. An edge of panic was digging me in the ribs and the voice of the snake was hissing, 'See, you will never be normal! You can't even move house without having the wobbles again!'

I felt as if I was adrift, somewhere in the middle of the Forth estuary, adrift in a tiny, insubstantial boat, no rudder, no engine, no map. Pulled by the tide, south to Edinburgh, north to Anstruther. Lost, drifting, alone. Cold, hungry and a bit scared.

Had we made a mistake? Was this the depression returning? Should we have stayed in Edinburgh safely tucked up in our contented, hard-earned comfort? Why did I think I had the courage to take on the world and win? I would be better to give in and just exist; anything is better that facing all this turmoil again.

Around this time I was developing an interest in art and someone gave me a copy of The Mysterious Boat by Odilon Redon[4]. As I looked at the painting I saw my own wee boat, the boat in my head, in my picture, my boat of despair in the middle of the Forth! Redon's boat was blue. If I had looked more closely at the image in my head, I am sure that my boat would have been blue too. In Redon's boat was a disconsolate figure sitting in the stern. It could have been an old man—or even a 'getting older' woman. She was just sitting there, making no attempt whatsoever to steer the boat in the right direction or any direction. Just sitting there, doing nothing at all. You really wanted to yell at her, 'you are in the shipping lane, you stupid woman, do something fast or you will be swimming with the fishes!'

Even as I was shouting this warning to the poor, painted sailor I was realising that in my head, my own

---

[4] http://www.odilon-redon.org/84458/The-Mysterious-Boat-large.jpg

image was waiting for me to look carefully at it and to see some interesting things. I also, was just sitting there. I wasn't moving anywhere. Was I also in the shipping lane, a sitting target for all the naval vessels moving out to sea from Rosyth? Perhaps it was time to take control and to decide on my direction.

But the Mysterious Boat wasn't called mysterious for nothing. If you look very closely at the stupid woman doing nothing in the stern you can see a shadow beside her. Ah-ha! A ghost? Plenty of sailors have been lost for ever in the Forth. An angel? I like that thought better. A heavenly presence sitting with me while I procrastinate, worry and forget to steer. I had forgotten that I could never be alone and without support on my journey; that God would send help and companionship, a presence to guide and encourage.

And was that boat really going nowhere? Not in the painting it wasn't. Redon's blue boat has a huge yellow sail full of the energy of a force 7. The wind has filled that sail and while the sailor looks forlorn and passive, that frail barque is being whisked along to somewhere. Who knows where?

The sea may be in turmoil. The sailor may be only just competent. The boat may be barely sea-worthy. But that mysterious presence makes the difference between drifting into a fog of depression or heading out to sea with confidence and a smile. Hurrah! Let's head for the open sea. Me, God (and Prozac), we can do anything together and succeed. I need to realise that the sea will always be turbulent, but learning to deal with the wildness is all part of the mysterious journey. And we don't travel it alone.

I love quotations and I found in my depression days that while I didn't have the concentration to read books, I enjoyed reading other people's wise thoughts, so long as they were no longer than two sentences. I guess I was also grasping at straws. Needing to find a way out of my prison I was hoping to find the key in one of these wise sayings.

I came to rely on them, the wise sayings of wise people, ancient and modern alike. They gave me strength and insight and often the courage I needed for the day.

Parts of the bible came to mean a lot to me, in particular the sayings of Jesus, the master healer, at a time when I really needed healing. Also, the Book of Psalms—in mornings of sheer, sharp panic or sometimes dead numbness I would turn to the book of Psalms and find there a man who seemed to have experienced many of my own struggles.

Listen to me, Lord, and answer me,
for I am helpless and weak. (Psalm 86:1)

His words became my words. I didn't have a vocabulary to say these things on my own.

Don't hide yourself from me!
Don't be angry with me;
don't turn your servant away.
You have been my help;
don't leave me, don't abandon me,
O God, my savior. (Psalm 27:9)

I felt so alone. If God also left there would be nobody. And feeling a total failure, I feared the anger of the world against me. They—whoever 'they' were— would be angry with me because I was stupid enough to be in this state. I needed God to believe in me or I would have no hope left.

And I needed to know that it was going to be all right—eventually, after I had slept well, after I had managed to pull myself together, after I got out of my pyjamas, after I managed to make the packed lunch. Eventually. Maybe next week.

I know that I will live to see the Lord's goodness in this present life. Said the Psalmist to me.

Trust in the Lord. Have faith. Do not despair. Trust in the LORD. (Psalm 27:13-14)

That man who wrote the Psalms sounds like a desperate man to me. He was a king, apparently, so I guess he would have many responsibilities and more than a few enemies. I didn't have any real enemies outside of myself although it felt like I did. The depression was MY enemy, filtering out anything good and health-giving and only allowing in the bleak sadness that I was beginning to think was the norm. But the sadness, the enemy within, was always working against me, and it felt like it was threatening my existence. So I resonated with the Psalmist.

> *Teach me, Lord, what you want me to do,*
> *and lead me along a safe path,*
> *because I have many enemies.*
> *Don't abandon me to my enemies,*
> *who attack me with lies and threats.*
> (Psalm 27:11-12)

At that time, my memory had gone, drowned by the depression along with deep sleep, concentration, healthy appetite and all other good things. So I resorted to writing everything down. I wrote down all my wise sayings and pasted them up in front of the kitchen sink so I could read them often throughout the day. Sometimes I stuck an odd quotation into a pocket so I could reach for it in a desperate moment in the supermarket. I took to writing a journal so I could make some sense out of my incomprehensible kangaroo thoughts. That journal became my best friend, the only thing that had the patience to soak up all my heaviness. Writing became a way of understanding myself. It was therapy.

Another tool I discovered was my imagination.

As a child, I lived in my fantasy world. I would sit on my swing, or halfway up a tree and dream for hour after happy hour. I played with dolls and wound elaborate stories around their little plastic bodies. I couldn't sleep at night for weaving myself into the stories I was reading or the programmes I had been watching on television. I became Dr Kildare's idol, the adored, terminally ill patient in Emergency Ward 10. I was the hero when the school went on fire. I was the favourite child of a rich banker with all the toys I could ever desire. I lived in an inner space, with my dreams and fantasies. And at this stressed time of my life I remembered the safety of that place and retreated there again.

But, as an adult, I found that my inner space was not filled with childish fantasy. It was still a haven, a retreat, a place of safety. But I began to realise that I wasn't alone there. Warmth, an enveloping, a tenderness that I can only assume was God, dwelt there also. At that point, I was incapable of loving myself and I was very busy rejecting the love of others. But there seemed to be an element of acceptance and love, intangible and unrecognised though it was, colouring that inner space.

One particular Easter was a really sad time for me. I had been really unwell, the depression lying so heavily on me I could hardly get out of bed. That was also the time of the horrible Dunblane massacre where so many five year olds were cruelly wiped out by a maniac's gun. I had taught in Dunblane Primary School for a time and I, along with most of the country, was devastated by these events.

On that Easter Sunday afternoon all three of my daughters were at home, then in their teens, happy to be off school or home from university and I felt I had to stay upstairs in my bedroom rather than be a miserable spectre at their feast. They were on holiday, enjoying being together again and had friends staying also. They were happy! I was such a misery!

So I escaped. A hurried 'I'll be back at teatime', an armful of books, my Bible and journal, which had become so important to me, and I was off. I took the car into the hills and wandered the country roads for a while. My ever faithful tears were my only companions but, when alone, it didn't matter so much that I was clearly unhappy. After a while, by that time hopelessly lost in the congestion of country lanes, I drew in to a quiet lay-by, slept for a while and woke to find myself crying—again. Nothing had happened to start the tears but I was sobbing as if my world had come to an end.

It was then that I opened my bible looking again to the Psalmist for help, gulping at the words, desperate for a breath of life. I was like a thirsty man in the desert. I needed water badly and I needed it that minute. And I found Psalm 40.

> *I waited patiently for the Lord's help;*
> *then he listened to me and heard my cry.*
> *He pulled me out of a dangerous pit,*
> *out of the deadly quicksand.*
> *He set me safely on a rock*
> *and made me secure.* (Psalm 40:1-2)

And I knew that my desperation was a cry to the Lord. I wasn't being patient in the least. I needed God to listen now, right now. I felt that I could cope with this no longer. I needed help and I needed it this minute. Something snapped inside. I yelled to God. Or maybe I just whimpered!

'God help me. Listen to me. I'm scared. I don't know what's happening to me. I have endured this as patiently as possible. I keep trying to get better. I try my best. But I'm scared that I will never get better. This is me – forever. I could die in this place and nobody would notice. In fact, maybe I'm dead already—Help me—please.'

And as I prayed and cried I saw a picture in my mind's eye. I saw a scrubby landscape among the hills. And I could see a female figure sitting on the ground beside a pool of thick, slimy mud. She was wearing beige linen trousers, just like mine, and a light shirt, the comfortable, shabby kind that we wear when nobody else is around. She looked very dejected. And I realised, of course, that this sad, curled-up figure was me. I was just sitting there, hugging my knees, head bowed, with no energy left to get up and walk away from the muddy hole. Experience had taught me that it wasn't worth trying to move on, climb the hill, find newness of life. There was no point. Every time I climbed laboriously to the top, I would just be picked up by some unseen force and be dropped down into the slime again. It was hopeless!

But here was the Psalmist telling me that he had been there too. And in his pain he also had cried out to the Lord and in his case God had intervened. God had pulled him out of the dangerous pit and had made him secure up the hill on a high rock. He was safe. No more mud for him. If God were making him secure then he really would be safe up there. He didn't need to worry any more.

Had I been an artist I would have painted that picture. But I committed it to memory and lived with it for months. I could imagine the pit of mud all too easily and identified it as the times of despair when I just couldn't believe in myself and felt completely worthless. I tried to picture a really safe, secure rock where I could again breathe freely and in doing so I remembered a visit to the Holy Land and to Masada, down in the desert overlooking the Dead Sea. Here on a plateau of 200 yards by 700 yards was where the ancient King Herod had built one of his winter palaces; a high secure place where he would be safe from all his enemies—and King Herod had a few! 1500 feet higher than the shores of the Dead Sea, this rock was absolutely immense.

From the top of Masada you can see for miles, right across the desert wilderness and barren mountains and to the east, over the Dead Sea. From that vantage point you could see armies marching towards you from twenty miles away. No one could catch you unawares. And the rock itself was so inaccessible that no one could reach you uninvited.

That place just felt different. Standing on the top, it seemed that the quality of light was different. The air had a mild fragrance, with a hint of eastern promise. You could almost touch the air. And the view was spectacular, painted in faint turquoise and pink and blue. It is the most beautiful place I have ever seen.

And so I chose my rock and imagined myself there, on top of Masada, with God's protection all around me, unseen but powerfully felt. This picture gave me peace.

> *He pulled me out of a dangerous pit,*
> *out of the deadly quicksand.*
> *He set me safely on a rock*
> *and made me secure.* (Psalm 40:2)

Pictures and images can be markers for our journey, secure points for us to hold on to and check our progress. My blue boat—the silent sailor trusting in the wind of the spirit. Words of scripture interpreted to us by its author gives us toeholds in the rocky road of life.

And now I had more tools for my journey, stacked away in my tool box—scripture, images and imagination. God had introduced me to each one.

To ponder:

An exercise:

Find a quiet space where you can be alone. Close your eyes, settle down and prepare to daydream.

Read and re-read this Psalm. Imagine it. Picture it. Imagine yourself within the picture. Feel the lostness of the slimy pit. Sit in that place in your imagination for a time.

Bit also, feel the lightness of being lifted out of the pit of despair. Feel the huge, safe hands that come to your rescue. Experience in your imagination the powerful security of these hands. And hear the voice that assures you of safety. Listen to the song around you in the air. And relax in this immense security. Turn your daydream into prayer.

> *I waited patiently for the Lord;*
> *he turned to me and heard my cry.*
> *He lifted me out of the slimy pit,*
> *out of the mud and mire;*
> *he set my feet on a rock*
> *and gave me a firm place to stand.*
> *He put a new song in my mouth,*
> *a hymn of praise to our God.*
> *Many will see and fear the Lord*

and put their trust in him.

Blessed is the one

who trusts in the Lord,

who does not look to the proud,

to those who turn aside to false gods.

Many, Lord my God,

are the wonders you have done,

the things you planned for us.

None can compare with you;

were I to speak and tell of your deeds,

they would be too many to declare.

(Psalm 40:1-5, NIV)

Chapter 10
Now

I had a distressing week and I had coped badly. All I wanted was to curl up beneath the duvet and stay there forever. I was fuzzy, weepy and drowning in the grey fog again. But I was committed to leading a silent retreat day at my favourite place of rest and so the strong bit of me insisted to the weepy bit of me that we go, however weepy and weak we were feeling.

So I got up early, took hours to decide what to wear so that I could be invisible, got into the car and headed north. All the time I was berating myself for being so stupid. How had I got myself into this emotional mess? Why could I not be like everybody else? Why did I cope so badly with things? Other people would take life's knocks, think it all through and move on. But me? No, I had to make a huge meal of every little disappointment, process it for a week, sleep for another week and then gradually put the pieces together again and get on with life. Stupid, stupid woman!

Then I moved from past and present weaknesses to the future. I would always be like this. I would never be any better. I was born stupid. I would never change. And I couldn't do it any more. I would have to give up everything and just stay at home and do nothing. I wasn't strong enough to live in this world. I just wanted to be normal.

It was late March—a brisk and breezy spring morning. As I crested the hill, the town of St Andrews appeared in front of me, flanked on two sides by the mighty North Sea, white horses absolutely galloping in to break into huge surf on the shore. It was breathtakingly beautiful. My driving became less than safe as I feasted my eyes on the sight, wanting to capture it and hold it in my memory, wallpaper my grey space with it and hold that moment in time forever.

The moment of glory reminded me that the sun still shines although I feel miserable. While I walk in corridors of grey it still rises each morning and the tide rushes in to shore twice a day. The beauty of the surf and shore, of daffodils in the grass, of a sleepy little stone-built town with ancient steeples and ruined towers, of fluffy March clouds scudding across a reinvented sky—this wonderful world still exists. But I have allowed myself to be imprisoned in my grey cell.

From there on I tried to notice the present moment and thanked God for everything I saw. Some trees were showing signs of a green haze, the start of their summer colours. There were daffodils everywhere. St Andrews was beautiful in its early morning stillness. Not a student in sight at this hour on a Saturday. Crossing the Tay I was aware of previous trauma and sadness when the old railway bridge had collapsed into the icy depths below—pain and distress yet people survive such tings. I can survive too.

The whole country was beautiful. How could I have missed all this in the last week of slumping in the fog? If I could only live in this present moment with all this beauty around me I would be fine. I could feel again. I might even feel happy.

It's called Mindfulness. Living in the present moment. It's so easy. No past recriminations, or regrets, or haunting memories. No worries about future plans and all that might go wrong. Living in the present moment is all about rejoicing and allowing ourselves just to be grateful. It brings lightness to our living and peace to our overworked and sad brains. And a spaciousness wherein we can be content.

It is a tool for cultivating contentment. All our constant striving leads to discontent. We are never good enough. We never will be good enough. But in this moment, this one moment, we are ok. We take time out from ourselves and from our negative voices to cultivate a spirit of gratitude and wonder. The present moment concentrates on what is right about a situation instead of what is wrong or missing.

When I go walking with children I am aware of walking 'mindfully'. It started when Skye was only a toddler without enough language to hold a proper conversation. So when we went for walks I would be looking carefully for objects around us to interest her. We had our routes around the estate where we lived at the time. Ronnie's garden had lovely little hedges, carefully cut into shapes of animals. We would admire them, stroke their heads, say goodbye to them and move on. Elinor's pond had frogs in it, popping their heads above the pondweed and croaking hello.

I would point out flowers, or birds, little things on the ground—sticks or flower petals or things people had dropped. Everything was a wonder to her. Her eyes sparkled as she pounced on the petals of a wind-blown rose and together we would gaze at its colours and feel its texture and see the beauty of colours merging into each other.

Adults never do that! Roses are red, or yellow or pink or whatever. They are just roses. But look at one carefully and be amazed at how intricately it is formed. And how did it get there? Who designed the rose? Who added its perfume? Why bother? We hardly notice! And yet, they are everywhere. For our enjoyment. For our pleasure. To fill up our senses. To help us enjoy living mindfully.

I walk mindfully on the seashore. We live in a beautiful part of the world here in east Fife and many stolen moments are spent beside the sea. Standing at the lighthouse or walking on the sand I get completely lost in the moment. The present moment. I love to beach comb, searching through the pebbles and seaweed to find today's treasures. What did the tide bring in today? Curly shells or driftwood. Pure white, smooth pebbles or roughened fragments of glass made beautiful by months in the surf.

In these moments, I get 'lost' in the moment. That moment. What is happening in that moment. Time slows. My heart rate slows. The past is distant and doesn't seem to matter. The future hasn't happened yet. There is only now, the present moment.

The other day I woke up in a haze of sadness. I wanted to curl down into the duvet and switch off my monkey mind and just cease to exist for a few hours. But the day was beautiful and the spring sunshine insisted that I got up and went exploring. I walked and walked until the glory of the day began to sink into my soul and my mind settled. I began to notice the world around me again and realised that all was well. My monkey mind had been lying to me. There was nothing scary out there. The world was beautiful. Actually, I was beautiful. There was no need for self-recrimination or self-hate or self-harassment. God was in charge of this lovely day. All was well.

Out on the rocks I watched the antics of the eider ducks and the shags. A grey heron had a run-in with a black-backed gull. I saw the first puffin of the season resting on its way to its nesting ground on the Isle of May. The tide was high. The sky was clear. The world was a beautiful place. I just need to notice that more often.

How can I make this a habit? We are much better at being mindless rather than mindful. Yet walking mindfully through the world feels healthy. It seems to bring lightness to my spirit and something approaching peace to my soul. It slows the heartbeat. It feels helpful and seems to be a way out of jail. It gets me out of my head, out of my obsessive thinking, away from gnawing worry and threatening anxieties. Everything feels less grey.

The aim of mindfulness is to bring a sense of order and calm to body and soul. Oh how I need that! It seems incredible then that we spend so much time complicating our lives with so much worry when we can easily restore the mind to simplicity, peace, and poise, and free it from confusion and distress.

In truth, mindfulness is taught by and has been an important part of all the major religions of the world. It is the fundamental human condition to need peace and simplicity in our lives. And so this need has been addressed and answers can be found, no matter what your spiritual convictions are.

So, with Jesus as my inspiration, I began to look at the gospels and traced Jesus' influence through history. I found it a fascinating path to follow. Here it is.

Jesus prayed. Why? Well, I don't really know the answers to that. But I can make guesses from what I read in the Gospels. He had a very close relationship with his father—God. The only way for him to make contact with God was through prayer. No emails, text messages or phone calls. He wanted to speak to his father, he had to pray. It was a love relationship. When we are away from home, we make contact with home or the office or the boyfriend or a son or a mother because we want to; because we miss the person we are phoning; because we need to talk something through with them, because we are worried; because we just want to hear the sound of their voice; because of a hundred reasons.

Jesus seemed to do the same and for all the same reasons.

Throughout the gospels we are told that Jesus went off to pray—on his own mostly. He got up early and escaped into the hills. After a hard day at the office, or his equivalent, he would need to leave the crowds behind and disappear off on his own. Often he would send his disciples across the lake to their next port of call and he would take time to get in touch with God. The night before his death, a time of utter aloneness when he needed more courage than the whole world had to give, he spent hours in prayer. What he heard or saw or experienced during these times we don't know. But he found them essential.

On one occasion when Jesus left his disciples and went on his own to pray, his poor, tired followers fell asleep. But when they awoke they were witness to something quite spectacular. They looked over to where Jesus had gone, making sure he was still there, and gasped in fright and utter astonishment. During that time of being with God, the mighty father figure, creator of the world and everything in it, Jesus had changed. Gone was the man they knew in his drab eastern robes and in his place stood someone totally transformed. He was shining white and glowing from head to toe. Not only that but he had two companions with him who just merged into the air after a time. This time with his father, God, had been a very special time when everything seemed different. Heavenly!

In the western world we do not expect prayer to be in any way even vaguely similar to that. In the Christian Church prayer usually takes the form of words— thousands and thousands of words. We bombast God with requests. We consider it good practice to tell him what we think he should do. We inform him about the people who need him—as if he didn't know already! And we think through a few human solutions to the world's problems and present them to God just in case he was stuck for answers.

How arrogant. Do we know this God at all? Do we think he can't run the world without our clever answers? Do we realise that without him we wouldn't have a brain to think through these answers? This is the God who created us, the one who masterminded the making of the universe, who breathed his own breath into our lungs and who welcomed us, mere humans, to walk on his earth! And we talk to him as though he were an equal?

Prayer at its best is transformational. It is a time when we sit at the feet of our maker and become more than we already are. We become what he has made us to be. We are HIS children. When we come to him in prayer we are welcomed as his little ones. He is pleased to have us there. This is relationship. This is love. And no words are necessary.

Call this meditation. Call it contemplation. Call it 'spacing out'. Call it what you want. The name is really unimportant. The fact is that this kind of prayer lets us rest in the present moment. It reminds us of the God who is. It renews our perception of ourselves as we are. It puts our lives into perspective.

It is not an end in itself. Usually we go on to talk, to thank, to ask, to renew our lives and our intentions. But it is actually all we need. A love relationship with our heavenly father. We may not change outwardly and become like an advert for a brand new soap powder. But internally we are glowing and sparkling and feel free and loved and we want to smile and be good to ourselves, to everyone we meet, to the world, the bus driver and even the neighbour's cat. We are free of ourselves and all that weighs us down.

When I am in the grey dungeon of depression, I avoid that place of prayer. It is the one thing that makes the difference to me, but I don't want to make the effort to go there. The strong part of me has to drag the weak part. Kicking and screaming and protesting, I come to prayer.

I breathe deeply, picturing each breath enter and leave my body. I imagine every breath as the breath of God, filling me full of goodness, bringing feeling and life to my dead interior. And I use my mantra as I breathe. 'The Lord is here. His spirit is with us.' My imagination sees his spirit fill me with life. And I get stronger as I sit there, at his feet, leaning on the throne of grace, basking in his presence.

The past disintegrates and seems to matter less. The future is yet to be. It can take care of itself. I am loved by this God. I need to know nothing more about the future than that he will be there ahead of me. So I need not worry. I only need to deal with this moment. And that is easy.

Living in the real world once I am grounded in the God world brings peace, simplicity, poise and energy. The knowledge that this present moment is filled with the presence of God makes this moment the only important one. The next moment will be special or not when it comes. But this moment is all I have right now. In this moment I am aware. In this moment I am good enough. In this moment I am strong.

Too good to be true?

Yes, it is too good to be true. But it is a glimpse of the perfect way to live. We can try it. We can practice. We can get better at it.

Yes, we will fail. We will often find ourselves burdened under a load of unreasonable anxiety about the future or recriminations about the past. The past and the future will want to stick their pins in us and worry us till the day we die.

The present moment will always be with us. We might miss it because of our obsession with past and future. But it is there to be lived, fully, mindfully, intentionally, and appreciatively. In the present moment we can feel grounded. We are not off flying kites in future skies. We are not fleeing the ghosts of past occurrences. We ARE. We just ARE. And life is good—right now. In this moment.

Find it in the tool box. A tool called 'mindfulness'.

To ponder:

The daily routine. Each day, make sure you do:

- something physical
- something creative
- something spiritual
- something intellectual

Being mindful. Take a few moments every hour to do the following.

- Stop what you are doing.
- Listen to whatever is going on. Note the sounds.

- Look around and SEE what is there.
- Choose something to concentrate on. Feel it, smell it, experience it in some way.
- Appreciate it.
- Appreciate the 'now moment'. Savour it. Thank God for it.
- Go back to what you were previously doing.

Chapter 11
The fourth dimension

According to Aristotle in the 4th century BC, there are only two ways of thinking and learning which are acceptable. The first is through what is experienced by the five senses and the second through logical deduction and induction. Over the years the world has come to accept this as fact and so this is how we build up our store of information. And so the world seems to have accepted that other forms of knowledge are therefore invalid or untrustworthy.

If Aristotle could visit the self-help department of any bookshop today he would be amazed to see the collection of widely read books on the occult, modern witch craft and all things 'new age'. And alongside these he would notice books on the lives of the saints and mystics through the centuries. He would also be fairly horrified at the resurgence of desire for knowledge about something altogether greater than logic, a something else, beyond and above the experience of ordinary living, another being, a higher power, the divine. The search is on, not for logical deduction and physical experience, but for mystical moments when ordinary individuals feel that they are in touch with God.

A summer evening; an hour before picking up children from Brownies; just time to walk the dog. The car park at Cramond looked the way it always did. The ground was still rough and stony. The trees were in the same place as always. Nothing had changed in the twelve hours since my last visit. I walked through the cars, down the slope, on to the foreshore, and my heart stopped.

The golden sunset had burst across the Forth, its delicate fingers wrapping up the hills, the sea, the boats, all before it, in tissue so light and iridescent that it took my breath away. I could only stop and stare. I don't know how long I stood there, mouth open, probably, in absolute awe. I had never seen anything so breathtakingly beautiful in the whole of my life.

It was a glimpse of Heaven. And in spite of my rush and the dog impatiently nipping at my heels, I felt the presence of God touch me, wordlessly, but with immense intensity. The sunset wasn't there for **me**. It probably wasn't there for **anyone** in particular. For the heavenly host this was nothing unusual. They would see such glory all the time. But for me it was a stolen peek into eternity. I could think of nothing to say but 'Wow!'

Afterwards, I rushed away, bundling the dog into the car, picking up children, attending to the bedtime routine, but I felt different. I could never 'unsee' that beauty, nor forget the touch of the Creator as I watched it. It was a mystical moment that changed me subtly, made me more aware of the greatness of eternity, just a sunset away.

Without knowing it, we long to touch base with a greater reality than logic or the intellect. We need to feel another life force, one that has pulsed on through the centuries and the light years and is still the throbbing heartbeat at the core of life—any life; all life; my life; your life.

In spite of the growth of science as the seeming foundation of all 21st century thinking, there are outbursts of total rebellion against all this rationalism. And so today, in every bookshop in the land there are cries for help from those who want to escape from this culture and find the 'new way' or rediscover an old one. The ancient ways of knowing are resurfacing with incredible and increasing energy. Every cry is screaming out that there has to be more to life than the quiet, tidy rationalism of Aristotle.

Imagine—an exhibition in York illustrating the medieval lifestyle of the people. At the end of a passageway I came across a wall-to-wall, floor to ceiling sheet of glass beyond which there was nothing. Well, almost nothing. I could only make out a few black boxes placed at random in the black-painted space beyond the smoked glass barrier. It seemed like the exhibition had strangely come to an abrupt end.

As I stood there wondering why, I saw a large button on the wall at the right hand side of the glass and a notice telling us to press it. Anticipating sliding doors to Aladdin's cave of medieval goodies I did as I was told and stood back, waiting. Nothing. The glass remained in place. The emptiness was total.

But wait. Look. So slowly as to be imperceptible, the black darkness beyond the veil was lifting. I had to blink. And blink again. Where once there was nothing, life had appeared—and disappeared. Did I see that? And there it was again. Flames flickering in a grate against one wall. A cobbler holding a...no, it had gone. I pressed the button again. Yes, it was there. A whole shop in front of my eyes. the cobbler making his shoes. A boy sitting on the floor working with a piece of leather. A woman with some...it had gone again.

For ten minutes the red button opened up this magic, long-gone world to me; a world un-noticed by the scurrying holiday maker intent on gobbling up fast fun but so solid and real to those enjoying every little moment in that place, those who took time to adjust their eyes to behold the new dimension. Invisible to the eyes of the uninitiated, but so clear, once you knew it was there.

And so is heaven as close to us as that? If only we know where to look and how to see we will become aware of another dimension—eternity and the present intermingling. The eternal now. Learning to live in the present moment and enjoying each unfolding minute in all its fullness, are we then able to experience a taste of heaven?

It's a bit like walking into a dark room. Your normal sight sees nothing. You are blind and the room is empty. But within seconds something happens in your wonderfully designed eyes. There's a silent click. Everything changes. You are in a new dimension. You can see in the dark. The longer you look the clearer it becomes. If you were to remain in that dark room for a long period of time you would see it all. It would become as clear as day.

'Earth's crammed with heaven and every common bush afire with God.'[5] But we need to 'see' things differently. In order to become aware of the

---

[5] Elizabeth Barrett Browning, Aurora Leigh: A Poem, London: J. Miller, 1864, Bk. VII, l. 812-826.

physical world and the heavenly world passing in and out of each other we have to experience that silent click. The one that changes our perception.

While still seeking recovery from depression, I attended a Celtic group for a while. At that time sleep was difficult for me, partly due to the lingering effects of the depression, but there were other reasons too. One evening we read a Celtic liturgy that asked for God, Christ and the Holy Spirit to lie down with us in our beds at night and for the angels to hover watchfully in the corners of the bedroom as we slept. Somehow I felt that this was important for me but wondered why.

I pictured my own cosy bedroom, and saw in my imagination that it was very crowded with angels sweeping around the ceiling and all these other holy entities keeping me safe, wrapped in my duvet. I had one startling, albeit imaginary, glimpse of my husband hanging off the edge of that very crowded mattress and shook inwardly with silent guffaws of laughter! But funny though it was, it showed me something more serious. Part of my problem about sleeping was the realisation of how scary it was for us all to sleep at the same time. How could I be in control of my world if everyone was asleep for the same six or seven hours? Help**!** **No one** was in control! Anything could happen!

Again I became aware of another world out there, another dimension. The founder of the Iona Community and famous Scottish Churchman prayed in this same way when he wrote the following,

> *In you God all things consist and hang together. The very atom is light energy, the grass is vibrant, the rocks pulsate. All is in flux; turn but a stone and an angel moves.'*[6]

I have become convinced of a deep 'inner knowing'. It is learning to live in the depths of this knowing that sustains us. It doesn't perhaps 'give us life' in the first place, but once we have found our depths we can sustain a kind if living that previously was impossible or, at best, spasmodic.

Throughout history, ordinary people living ordinary lives have discovered this deep inner knowing and have become more truly themselves through this discovery. It has gradually changed them from manic, anxiety-driven, workaholic people-pleasers to calm, focused stable contented individuals, comfortable in their own skin. They have come home. They have learned to 'abide in the presence'. Busy but

---

[6] *Man is made to rise* written by the Very Rev Dr George Fielden MacLeod

composed, active but connected, mostly joyful, often serene, occasionally harassed but easily reconnected.

....we must fly to our beloved homeland. There the Father is and there is everything. [7]

They include the saints in the Christian tradition. They are gurus and mystics, in wider belief systems. The Desert Fathers, the Celtic saints, the Sufis, all testify to the deep inner knowing of being at home within one's self in the company of the great creator, the 'something more' or the 4th dimension.

I wonder if we came into this world with knowledge of this 'inner knowing'. Created by the master creator, moulded, carved and chiselled into being by powers beyond our outer experience, nurtured in the womb by love from beyond this world. Did we experience the presence of God before we were even born?

My first grandchild, Skye, was born less than two years after my father's death. When she was old enough to notice things I used to carry her in my arms and show her all the family photographs hanging on the walls of my staircase. Without fail she would point

---

[7] St Augustine, The City of God, 5th Century AD, De Civitate Dei translated into English

to the photo of my father, almost as if she was telling me that she recognized him and was pleased to see him again.

Fanciful? Perhaps. But it does make me wonder. What if...? What if we do come from heaven in the first place? What if we are handcrafted and designed by a master's hand and loved into being? What if we are children of heaven first and foremost and we live out our earthly lives far from our natural comfort zone? Rooted in heaven, but growing in the world?

And what if that same God moves in and through this world not just occasionally but every moment of every day? What if he really did make me, handcrafted me, knows me outside in and through and through? What if he is as interested in my life and well being as I am in that of my daughters? What if he loves me as much as I love them? What if he is always aware of and concerned about life, all my petty anxieties and worries, all the major dramas and problems? What if...?

That might explain why we find that we 'come home' to God when we get in touch with our depths and glimpse the shadow of the umbilical cord. Our 'inner knowing' hears the call of that natural home where we were most truly ourselves, long before we learned to wear the mask to cope with the world. We came from God. Our lives will be richer when we 'see' and experience the eternal dimension where we live in the presence of the angels.

I have a friend who came out her house one morning, locked the door of her top-floor flat, said good morning to the tall guy standing on the landing and went off to work. On her way down the stairs she heard herself say, 'That was a really tall angel.' Her conscious mind hadn't immediately realised that the tall guy on the landing was about 7'6' and dressed like a Roman soldier. But the less rational part of her that slips in and out of the 4th dimension had a kind of inner knowing. That had been an angel. Her flat would be safe in spite of the present local crime wave.

The ancient Celts believed that God was in the air we breathe. If that is the case then we are full of God. Each of us is full of God. Each of us can breathe in heaven as easily as we can breathe on earth. If the eyes of our hearts are open we can see heavenly things as clearly as we can see earthly things. We can see the things of God and we can see the things of the world. A unity that holds all things together.

The 4th dimension is the God dimension—where we live with miracle and wonder and an openness to the pedestrian becoming shot through with pure gold. God in all things. Heaven and earth sliding in and out of each other, overlapping, intermingling, glory and reality alive and well and existing in one life. My life.

Your life. God in us. Clothing us in pure gold and breathing his energy into our dullness.

If it was in tablet form we would be demanding it—the miracle drug. Beware. Side effects include contentment and possible happiness; could cause feelings of self -worth.

Life in the 4th dimension. Life in all its fullness.

To ponder:

A Celtic prayer. Use it often to surround yourself with the love and the power that God promises us.

My shield, my defender, my Christ.
For each day, each night, each dark, each light,
My shield, my defender, my Christ.

Chapter 12
It's not worth it!

I was a mess. I felt tired all the time. I was angry. I was so sad that tears were always waiting to be beckoned. My life took over the real me. I was lost in it. In its busyness, its constant demands, its weary grind. My children, lovely as they were, seemed to take up so much of my energy, both mental and physical. A busy manse echoed to the sound of the doorbell, the kettle, meetings, and parishioners dropping in. People were ill, in need, distressed. Or they were anxious, angry, wanting to vent frustration or looking for clarification. Life was relentless. And time was lost in whirling activity.

On the surface I was coping. People said that I was always cheerful and helpful. Always ready to listen and be kind. 'HA!' I would think. 'If only they knew what was really going on inside my head!' Inside I was angry. Other young mums had the luxury of bringing up their children in peace. They had time to enjoy their children, to play with them and to spend quality time with them. I had a whole parish to keep me from mine and they seemed to get swallowed up in the whirlwind that was our home life. When I fell in love with my own Prince Charming I didn't sign up for this!

I ranted. At the parish, yes. But I ranted at my children also. They were the victims of this manic lifestyle, but somehow I felt that if they were easier, less demanding, dirtied fewer clothes and didn't need to be fed three times a day, then and only then would I be able to cope. And I was angry with my husband. If he hadn't been so committed to the people of his parish then he would be a better husband, spend more time helping me and listening to me and being there to bath little bodies and put them to bed and read bedtime stories.

And I was angry at God. I wasn't fit for all this. I wasn't a strong person either physically or mentally and here he was asking me to carry a very heavy load of responsibility. Surely he knew I couldn't do this on my own. I needed an army of helpers—which I didn't have!—to get through each day. It was his fault. He expected too much of me!

I remember coming downstairs one summer evening after putting all three girls to bed. The kitchen had disappeared under the detritus of dinner preparation and dirty dishes. Tomato ketchup was smeared over two thirds of the table and the rice pudding had boiled over on the hob. I closed the door on it all and went in to the living room. It was as bad. Toys everywhere and not a chair clear enough to sit on. The low summer sun was illuminating a pink and purple patch of 'My little ponies' and I sank on the floor and hugged them as I began to pack them into the toy box. Why was life so hard, I asked myself?

And then I cuddled down on the floor in the evening sunshine and cried. I couldn't cope any longer. I didn't have the energy for another day. It wasn't worth it. This life was too much.

After a while I reached over to the bookcase and got my Bible out. The Psalms, I was told, answered every problem you could ever have. So, to the Psalms I turned. And at random I picked out Psalm 32,

> *Happy are those whose sins are forgiven, whose wrongs are pardoned.*
> *Happy is the one whom the LORD does not accuse of doing wrong and who is free from all deceit.*
> *When I did not confess my sins, I was worn out from crying all day long. Day and night you punished me, LORD; my strength was completely drained, as moisture is dried up by the summer heat.* (Psalm 32:1-4)

This wasn't the message I had wanted to hear. I was hoping for God to say, 'Don't worry Dorothy. I will sort out all these people who are bothering you. And I will give you a slave to do all your work. And I will put a barrier around your house so nobody will ever visit again. And I will make your daughters like little perfect puppets and you will never have to feed or bath them. And I will turn your husband into a meek and mild version of himself and all he will ever want to do is look after you.'

Oh yes. That's what I wanted to hear. But as I read these words from Psalm 32 I was moved. And reduced to even more tears. And I knew that what I really needed to do was have a long look at my life and confess my sin and my shortcomings—and my anger; and my envy; and sloth; and deceit; and hopelessness. There was plenty to bring to God. He knew already of course but he wanted me to become aware of my sin and to bring the mess of life to him.

That night was a turning point. When I finally cried out all my failings and my inability to cope with this life—a life I had always wanted to live incidentally, with husband, babies, a parish and the 'vocation' of being a servant to the parish—I began to feel better. I calmed down, dried the latest tears and began to read again.

Then I confessed my sins to you; I did not conceal my wrongdoings. I decided to confess them to you, and you forgave all my sins. So all your loyal people should pray to you in times of need. When a great flood of trouble comes rushing in, it will not reach them.

You are my hiding place; you will save me from trouble. I sing aloud of your salvation, because you protect me. (Psalm 32: 5-7)

And so with the assurance that God was my safe place, my hiding place and that he would rescue me from trouble, I was able to face the rest of the day and the kitchen and the chaos of the toy-strewn room.

We seem to be hard-wired for God. It's as though there is an invisible and extremely far stretching umbilical cord between him and each one of us and if we stray too far from him we become distressed. Then it's time to creep in again and have time with our creator to confess our wanderings and our insufficiency and renew our strength.

'Sin' is not a popular word in the 21st century, but it is as real and as lethal as it always has been. Facing up to the fact that we are sinners is hard. Finding words to confess the sin is hard. Even recognising what sin is, is hard. But if we don't take it seriously then the psalmist warns us what will happen.

When I did not confess my sins, I was worn out from crying all day long. Day and night you punished me, LORD; my strength was completely drained, as moisture is dried up by the summer heat. (Psalm 32:3,4)

We probably all know people who have become bitter and twisted over the years. They have as much and as little to complain about as the rest of us. But these people have chosen to inhabit their sin—the sin of envying others, the sin of anger against God or other people, the sin of fearfulness, the sin of laziness, the sin of greed, wanting more and more in the hope that eventually they might feel satisfied. They inhabit their sin as a habit of mind. Easier to flow in the river of blame and negativity than it is to examine themselves and climb on to the bank to get a better view of their situation.

That's what I had done that summer long ago. It was easier for me to blame everybody else for my sadness than it was to confess my sin. It was the fault of the parish that I was so overwhelmed. It was my husband's fault. It was the fault of the children. It was the fault of everybody! And I flowed easily in that negative and poisonous river. Until the day that the Psalmist told me to confess my sin. It was that easy. I just had to take a long hard look at my attitudes and confess them to the God who knows how I operate best. And he made me better. At least, for a time!

But what is sin and how do we recognise it in our lives?

In the 4th century a man named Evagrius lived in Pontus in the Black Sea area of Turkey. He went on to become one of the Desert fathers, living the life of a hermit in the Egyptian desert. Evagrius' teachings on asceticism, prayer, and the spiritual life had a profound impact upon the young Christian world. I guess that nowadays he would be known as a psychotherapist and life coach or spiritual director. Evagrius has gone down in history as the man who invented the seven deadly sins! It would be more accurate to say that he began to recognise and give names to seven, sometimes eight or even nine habits of mind or thoughts that were sinful. He called them 'logismoi' or vices. Here they are:

vainglory
Anger
gluttony
sadness
avarice acedia
pride
fornication

If I could add to the list I would add:

fear
envy

So there we have a list of habits of mind that bring us grief and become our 'vices'. I am sure that like most of us, you will be able to do all the sins perfectly well without needing lessons. But I think that each of us has a dominant sin. We are guilty of them all. But some are more persistent that others. It seems helpful to us if we can isolate the sins that get us down the most so that we can tackle them and confess them. And this should bring healing to us and rest for our souls.

A sin is a habit, an action or a way of being that stops us from being the best that we could be. If God created each one of us, handcrafted our bodies and our souls in the womb, then he already sees the life I am designed for. A habit or an action that wastes away my potential is harmful to me and represents a turning away from God. These habits become vices when they take over my way of life and stop my growth into the human being that God means me to be. It'd be like having a little dose of poison for breakfast every day. It makes us ill.

I have discovered that my most persistent sin is 'acedia'. This is a concept that we have mostly lost sight of these days so let me give you an idea of its meaning. Acedia is a Greek word that names a state of languor or torpor. It speaks of an unconcern or dissatisfaction with one's condition—or dissatisfaction with anything we do. It speaks to me of laziness, cynicism, an attitude of 'I don't care about anything' that seeps through my bones till I can do nothing but complain and sleep. It is heavy. It is like anaesthetic. It numbs the body and the soul and reduces a once vibrant person to a couch potato with attitude. I am that couch-potato on my worst days.

When acedia takes control I am not always aware at first that my feelings have become dampened because by that time I have become disconnected from my feelings. I can become vague and undefined, as if I wasn't actually there. I have disappeared into myself and am lost to the world. It is a half-life, there in my acedia. People ask me what I'm feeling and I shrug and say I don't know. And I don't. My feelings have been taken over by the anaesthetic—or the acedia—and I am just a heavy, vague shell. Then I will space out with television or reading or sleeping, waiting, just waiting to get my life back when all this passes.

When I was depressed I lived in this world most of the time. My other dominant sin at that time was fear, making me a hotchpotch of anxiety that wouldn't speak for hours on end because I had lost myself in the ocean of scariness that was the inside of my brain.

Anger? Oh yes! I could do that fairly well also. Nothing is as it should be, including myself. Of course I was wrapped up in anger about the state of things and the state of the people who shared life with me. And how I disliked myself! I was angry about how unlovable I was in the midst of it all. But mostly I took my anger out on other people.

Pride? Not so much so. There isn't much to like in myself and less to feel proud about. But pride is a sin and will always be lurking around somewhere.

Vainglory. What is that? The dictionary would define it as an excessive or ostentatious pride especially in one's own achievements or abilities—or a boastful vanity, or empty pomp and show. When I am ill there is little vainglory in my life. But when I am functioning well and life is good I can find myself indulging in this. I love the feeling of achievement and there's nothing wrong with that. I love to work hard and enjoy the rewards and the affirmation from people. But I guess I have to watch that I don't just go for the affirmation or for the glow of achievement. And it is always a temptation to feel good but to be living a lie in order to get the feeling. So yes, I CAN do vainglory!

Sadness? Yes Mr Evagrius, I can do sadness. Anyone who is of a depressive turn of mind can do sadness far too easily. It is a huge temptation which I have to resist daily. It is the place I go as soon as tiredness sets in. It feels comfortable and I quite like it there because I know it so well. But no one else likes me there. They only get half the person I am and a grumpy half at that. So Lord, please forgive my sadness especially when it cuts me off from the rest of the world and turns me into a grumpy recluse.

Avarice. Is that what I do when I park three miles from the shops instead of paying for a parking ticket? Or when I hole up in my house instead of joining everyone else at a function. Sometimes, just sometimes, I realise that I am keeping myself to myself. And I am keeping my stuff to myself, along with my knowledge, my presence, and my time. It is selfish. It doesn't actually make me feel any better. And it makes me less of the person that I really am. I really am better without this stingy corner of my nature taking control of me.

And gluttony, fornication or lust? At this moment, as I fight to lose a few pounds after the Christmas feasting, I recognise my gluttony. And do we all indulge in a little 'fornication' but call it something else? And envy. Do we just call it 'wishing'? If only I had a degree from Oxford, then my life would be fine! If only I hadn't been born in the countryside, I would be more successful by now! If only I was as attractive as my sister I would have had a more successful life!

And fear? How much anxiety swishes around our every thought. It makes us over-cautious and scared and stops us from doing the best we can.

We were designed and created by the one who engineered the big bang, the one who threw the planets into orbit and designed the beauty of the humble little daisy. We are designed to be fabulous! But sin comes in like a virus and wastes the beauty and magnificence of the successful outcome. But we don't need to let that happen. We are given a procedure. We are given access to the designer. We have an 'out of jail' card and it's called forgiveness. The God who designed and created us loves us enough to give us a second chance, and a third, and fourth.

So it is worth taking our sin seriously.

The second clause in the 'out of jail' card is that we must also forgive the ones who have sinned against us. You know who they are in your life! And I had a list too. In my recovery from depression I started to build a picture of what had been going on inside me and how the refusal to forgive other people was spoiling my every waking day.

Inside me I had created a great big pot. In my imagination it was a huge terracotta urn with a tight-fitting lid and it sat somewhere in the region of my heart. Every time someone hurt me I would lift the lid and pop in all the hurt that I felt. This pot filled up quite quickly. But still I squeezed into it all the emotion that life brought up that I couldn't cope with. Soon I was having to stuff these hurts and angers and fears into the pot and actually sit on the top of the pot to keep the lid on it. Otherwise my pot would have been overflowing and messy. In my naivety I thought I was doing the best thing. Better to bury all these dangerous things. They could do untold damage if allowed out into the world.

But, of course, like all buried poisonous waste, it seeps out and slowly erodes the world that we want to so carefully protect.

I have a dear friend who is currently jeopardising her future by holding grudges about her childhood; failing to deal with the hurts from her past that are locked up in her big pot. Her career is important to her and hasn't gone to plan. She fears that she will not be the success she has always wanted to be. It is true that she is very talented in her profession and is becoming highly sought-after in a slightly different way from the fantasy of her childhood. But her hurts are reigning just now. If her parents had treated her differently she would have had a better chance. If her schooling had only been better. If she had grown up in the city instead of her little provincial town. If she had better financial resources. If she had a posher accent. If ... And so her hurts have power over her. She IS a success. She has done VERY, well in a particularly difficult field of work. She is amazing in my eyes and in the eyes of many people.

But she is nursing her little bundle of hurts, keeping them in ship-shape order. And the hurts are growing poisonous spores that are leaking out and wasting her beautiful soul and what might still become a beautiful life. Her pain is seeping out of that big pot and having a devastating effect on her happiness and contentment.

But what are our options? What can we do with all the hurts that life throws at us? They inevitably have an effect on us. Some of us are more resilient than others and can forgive, learn the lesson and move on. Most of us can't. And most of us have no idea where to start.

I confess to being one of these people. I took my little bundle of hurts and blamed my mother. Almost everything was her fault. If she had loved me as much as she loved my sister...If she had taken the time to read stories to me...If she had taught me how to look after my money...If she had given me encouragement instead of lectures.

These were the reasons why I couldn't be happy. The reasons for my depression. It was HER fault really. And so I was absolved of responsibility. Being a failure in life was all her fault and not mine so I spent my energy on refusing to take responsibility for my own life. And how could I ever forgive her? Her sins against me were immense. I am the victim here! So it is no wonder that I am a mess. It is NOT MY fault. Wrong again Dorothy. My fault here is refusing to move on from what I saw as a bad start in life. I need to take responsibility for the rest of my life. It is up to me. Am I going to sit here with my lump of resentment for company? Or am I going to move on and make my life something to be proud of?

But it is much harder than it sounds on paper! To move on we need to look our resentments in the eye. Acknowledge these hurts and our own reactions to them. Then we have a choice. Do we forgive the people involved or do we hang on to our toxic bundle till we die of toxaemia? Not an easy choice when we are in the midst of the pain.

Would it be easier to put the lid back on the pot and sit ever more firmly on it so that we can ignore our resentments? No, because the poison is already affecting our attitudes and our happiness.

Would it be easier to remain a victim and make a career out of blaming anyone and everyone and remaining 'stuck' in our uncomfortable rut?

Or we could just slip into denial and forget it all? Sounds more positive perhaps but just look at the consequences. Denial also has its poison and it works at a deep level. Our hurt might be stuffed deep in the pot and out of sight. But its slow, corroding vandalism comes to consciousness in our dreams and in a slowly crumbling foundation. Eventually our world begins to fall apart.

Or should we take a deep breath, list our grievances and take a long hard look at them. That thought may feel overwhelming. What do we do with all this hurt if we let it out of the pot? It is full of the puss of a rancid ulcer that has suppurated in the dark for far too long, unattended to. The one thing we must NOT do is stick it back in again out of terror and panic. It has to be faced. Nothing can be healed if we don't recognise that there is a problem. The sores need to be looked at, cleaned out and tenderly cared for until the new skin grows and the pain subsides and healing happens. This is possible. It can be done. But it takes courage. And do we have that courage?

Another tool; perhaps the brightest and best in the toolbox. Forgiveness.

To ponder:

In dealing with deep hurts you may find it helpful to find a counsellor or soul-friend to listen to you and to sit with you. But if you decide to do this alone, please remember to be gentle on yourself. The Father who made us loves us unconditionally is ready to listen kindly to you. He wants you to be healed and encourages you to draw close to him.

Create a quiet, safe place where you can be alone. Take a notebook and pen and a big scarf.

Sit comfortably in this safe place and ask God to join you.

When you feel ready, imagine that you take out the pot from your heart, the one full of resentment and hurt, and place it by your side. In YOUR imagination it might be a wooden crate, or a cardboard box. Whatever it is, imagine that you have it beside you.

Ask God to go with you as you begin the task of unpacking it.

For today, just take out one hurt. There are many days ahead to deal with the others.

Look at it. Retell the incident. List the hurts and the emotions. List the thoughts surrounding the hurt.

Name the people involved. Try to answer the question, 'What have I lost because of this incident?'

When you feel overwhelmed, ask God to draw near to you and give you courage. Use the big scarf to wrap around yourself so you feel enclosed and safe.

In your journal or notebook, write your rant. Rant about the incident allowing yourself to give free vent to all the emotion of the years that is being released. All your anger, anxieties, fears, sadness, and your regrets.—take them out of the pot and lay them down at your feet.

Use a verse of scripture, a word from God, to help you dig out all the poison.

Cry, if you can. Rage, if you can. Give full rein to the locked-up emotion that now rushes to meet you.

Hand it all over to God. Keep nothing back. Ask for forgiveness for your own part and try to better understand the person who hurt you.

Then leave it for a while. Visit your safe and sacred place often and discuss the matter further with your Heavenly Father.

Well done. Spring cleaning has begun. And remember—the Lord is here. His Spirit is with us. You will never be alone.

Chapter 13
Making sense of life

This book has been all about losing and finding. To put it dramatically, I lost my life to depression—at least for a few years. And sadly, it will always be the spectre at my feast. It could—and does—return at any time. It seems to be part of my 'make-up', one of the challenges that God has built in to my nature, one of the little extras he gave me while I was still growing in the womb.

And it has been about finding. Finding ways of living that challenge the depression; finding the tools to cope with a depressive nature; finding some of the answers God built into my psyche when he allowed my nature to be inclined towards depression.

It seems that we spend the first part of life, however long or short a time, optimistically pushing ahead in the hope that life will be good, we will love and be loved and that success, whatever colour it may be, will be just around the corner. It is part of the challenge of living to discover that it isn't as easy as that. There are forces at work to destroy our illusions, challenge our assumptions and demand that we alter our way of handling our world. That is when we need a route map! Or at least, a chat with the one who sees the way through the fog.

Not everyone immediately recognises a significant loss in their lives when it happens. Sometimes it is as obvious as bereavement or redundancy or divorce. Other times it is much more subtle. Feeling ostracised, alone or misunderstood. Moving house or town or job—even a happy decision to move on can bring about the feelings of disconnection. Or it might be memories of the past coming back to sit like a damp cloth on your happiness. Or feeling under-used and empty, feeling over- stretched or tense.

Often the first signs are feeling blue. I meet people all the time who just feel jaded and feel that nothing satisfies any more. And they are asking 'sad' questions. 'What's it all about anyway? What's the point? Nothing seems all that important any more. Why is that? Have I done something wrong?' They are bored and they don't seem to have the energy to make the changes that would bring them back to life.

Some of us have so little insight into ourselves that we just refuse to look at a deeper level for answers. We think that we should just get on, don't think about it, ignore the bleakness, and it will all just go away. Some people—and I would have been one of them before the depression—think that 'wobblies' only happen to unstable people whose outlook on life is flawed. They are just 'weirdos' and we want nothing to do with them.

But when nothing satisfies and there seem to be no answers within our own experience of life, what is there to do? It's like being at sea in a nice little boat that has always been reliable and safe for years and years. But suddenly a wave comes along and turns the boat over, spilling our whole life out to be dispersed by the waves, leaving us clinging to the upturned boat. It was so cosily familiar that we hadn't noticed that the boat had become worn-out and damaged and was no longer fit-for-purpose.

When that kind of disaster happens we have two options: We can hang on to the unturned but wrecked boat—frantically hoping that it will miraculously turn into something wonderfully new and sparkling. Or we can give ourselves up to the tide, turn ourselves in the right direction and allow ourselves to be borne on the waves till we begin to see where we are going again.

The second option is a risky strategy! We might never make it to shore and we may be swept way off course. But, let's face it; hanging on to the upturned boat is hardly a fail-safe method of finding new life either. If we hang on long enough we might possibly, eventually, wash up with the tide on some random shore where we can pick up our old lifestyle once again. But more likely we will be nibbled at by the fishes and, just before drowning, see our lives flash before us or end up reminiscing fondly on the way things used to be.

Change. We all hate it. But no one can avoid it. And God can use it to change us from the kitchen maid into Cinderella, from the wee country boy into the Lord Mayor of London—If we let Him, and if we go for option 2.

So let's do it then. Let's go for option 2 and learn how to ride the waves. It will mean dropping many of our old patterns of thought. Making qualitative judgements will have to go. Sticking rigidly to how we came to view the world, God and ourselves. That will also have to be reassessed. We may have to forgive people from the past who have wronged us. We may have to forgive ourselves, an even harder task.

Are we willing to make a fresh start within ourselves? Start noticing our emotions and how they affect our happiness? Begin to look for the mystical among the everyday activity? Try out different ways of prayer and put ourselves into unusual places of grace where we might just experience the 'something more' moments? Use our imagination to explore our relationship with our Heavenly Father. And practise sitting at the feet of the great creator who longs for our company and glories in our presence.

I hope the richness of the future will be worth the trials of the journey. I leave you with a prayer from Philip Newell.

At the beginning of time and at the end
You are God and I bless you.
At my birth and in my dying
in the opening of the day and at its close,
in my waking and my sleeping
You are God and I bless you.
You are the first and the last,
the giver of every gift,
the presence without whom there would be no present,
the life without whom there is no life.
Lead me to the heart of life's treasure
that I may be a bearer of the gift.
Lead me to the heart of the present
that I may be a sharer of your eternal presence.[8]

---

[8] 'Lead me to the heart of the present' from *Sounds of the Eternal: A Celtic Psalter*, J. Philip Newell, 2003 Canterbury Press, p76, Used with permission.